PENGUIN CLASSICS

P9-CDZ-996

TWO LIVES OF CHARLEMAGNE

EINHARD was born of noble parents in the Main valley around
AD 770. He was educated at the monastery of Fulda, and was sent
in the 790s to the court of Charlemagne. He became a friend of
Charlemagne and his family, and was chosen to invite Charlemagne to crown his son Louis the Pious as his successor in 813.
After Charlemagne's death he was a loyal servant of Louis the
Pious, both in Aachen and on his estates at Seligenstadt, where he
died in 840. In addition to the *Life of Charlemagne*, probably
written in 826–7, we have letters to and from Einhard, his account
of the *Translation of the Relics of Marcellinus and Peter* (830)
and *On the Adoration of the Cross*.

NOTKER BALBULUS (Notker the Stammerer) was born near the
monastery of St Gall, in Switzerland, around 840, and entered
the monastery as a boy. He wrote his account of Charlemagne
for the emperor Charles the Fat between 884 and 887. He also
composed a book of sequences with music, a *Martyrology* (896),
and poems, letters and charters. He taught at the monastic school
until his death in 912.

DAVID GANZ is Professor of Palaeography at King's College,
London. He studied history at Oxford and wrote a thesis on the
Carolingian monastery of Corbie. He taught medieval Latin at
the University of North Carolina at Chapel Hill from 1980 to
1996 and has published articles and chapters on Carolingian
intellectual history and on early medieval manuscripts and
libraries.

EINHARD *and*
NOTKER THE
STAMMERER

Two Lives of Charlemagne

Translated with an Introduction and Notes by
DAVID GANZ

PENGUIN BOOKS

PENGUIN CLASSICS

Published by the Penguin Group
Penguin Books Ltd, 80 Strand, London WC2R ORL, England
Penguin Group (USA) Inc., 375 Hudson Street, New York, New York 10014, USA
Penguin Group (Canada), 90 Eglinton Avenue East, Suite 700, Toronto, Ontario, Canada M4P 2Y3
(a division of Pearson Penguin Canada Inc.)
Penguin Ireland, 25 St Stephen's Green, Dublin 2, Ireland
(a division of Penguin Books Ltd)
Penguin Group (Australia), 250 Camberwell Road, Camberwell, Victoria 3124, Australia
(a division of Pearson Australia Group Pty Ltd)
Penguin Books India Pvt Ltd, 11 Community Centre, Panchsheel Park, New Delhi – 110 017, India
Penguin Group (NZ), 67 Apollo Drive, Rosedale, North Shore 0632, New Zealand
(a division of Pearson New Zealand Ltd)
Penguin Books (South Africa) (Pty) Ltd, 24 Sturdee Avenue, Rosebank, Johannesburg 2196, South Africa

Penguin Books Ltd, Registered Offices: 80 Strand, London WC2R ORL, England

www.penguin.com

First published in Penguin Classics 2008

026

Translation and editorial matter copyright © David Ganz, 2008
All rights reserved

The moral right of the translator has been asserted

Set in 10.25/12.25 pt PostScript Adobe Sabon
Typeset by Rowland Phototypesetting Ltd, Bury St Edmunds, Suffolk
Printed and bound in Great Britain by Clays Ltd, Elcograf S.p.A.

ISBN: 978-0-140-45505-2

www.greenpenguin.co.uk

Contents

Acknowledgements

This new translation of the ninth-century Lives of Charlemagne by Einhard and Notker the Stammerer was made at the suggestion of Rosamond McKitterick. It was written during my stay at the Netherlands Institute of Advanced Study, close to the heartlands of Charlemagne's empire, where I had the benefit of advice from three excellent Carolingian scholars, Mayke de Jong, Rosamond McKitterick and Els Rose, and the generous wit and wisdom of Jan Ziolkowski. In addition I have been able to consult Janet Nelson and Stuart Airlie. Paul Dutton's learning and kindness, and his profound knowledge of Einhard, have been a continual support. Dr Matthias Tischler, whose study of the manuscripts of Einhard's Life has transformed our understanding of that text, has been generous with his advice. We await his new edition of the Latin text. The person who has taught me most about Notker is my wife, Susan Rankin.

I have been worrying about Einhard and Notker since I first read them as a student in 1970, and I should like to dedicate this translation to the memory of the two friends whom I should most like to have read and improved it, Donald Bullough and Patrick Wormald. I am most grateful to Marcella Edwards at Penguin for all her help, and to Elizabeth Stratford for her outstanding copy-editorial assistance.

General Introduction

In May of the year 1000 the 20-year-old emperor Otto III visited Aachen and opened the tomb of the emperor Charlemagne, taking one of his teeth, trimming his nails and replacing the tip of his nose, which had decayed, with gold. Otto had adopted Charlemagne's slogan of 'renewal of the Roman empire' on his seals; his visit may well have been the prelude to an attempt to make Charlemagne a saint. For Otto, Charlemagne was the heroic predecessor who served as a model of what an emperor should be, an image for which he drew on Einhard's biography. This was already an established tradition: Charlemagne's grandson Charles the Bald had not only been given his name, he had frequently been urged to imitate his heroic ancestor. Throughout the Middle Ages Charlemagne was celebrated as a hero, the central figure of a large number of epic poems composed all over Europe. At the Battle of Hastings in 1066 a Norman minstrel sang of Charlemagne and Roland. In 1165, at the prompting of the emperor Frederick Barbarossa, Charlemagne was made a saint, and in 1215 his bones were placed in a golden reliquary at Aachen by the emperor Frederick II, with Frederick himself securing the last nail in place. Other twelfth-century authors made him a key figure in the Christian reconquest of Spain and the fight against Islam, and as the heroic ancestor of the kings of France. The poet Giles of Paris wrote a Latin epic about Charlemagne in five books in around 1200 to provide Louis, the son and heir of Philip Augustus, with a model to emulate. In Canto XVIII of the *Paradiso*, Charlemagne appears to Dante in the sixth heaven. Historians asserted that he was rightly called 'the Great' just like Alexander or Pompey and described his gigantic appearance. Joan of Arc believed that St Charlemagne had helped her to raise the siege of Orléans.

Charlemagne inspired later rulers: in 1681 the French bishop and historian Bossuet compared him to Louis XIV. Napoleon visited Charlemagne's tomb in 1804 before his coronation, and in 1809, resisting the independent stance of French bishops he stated: 'I am Charlemagne.' From 1950 the Charlemagne Prize has been awarded by the city of Aachen for distinguished service on behalf of European unification. Among those who have received the award are Jean Monnet, Konrad Adenauer, Winston Churchill, George Marshall, Henry Kissinger, Tony Blair and Bill Clinton, together with ministers and presidents of the European Commission. So Charlemagne is still an emblematic figure in the construction of contemporary Europe.

Charlemagne was the eldest son of Pippin, a Frankish noble who was hereditary mayor of the palace to the last Merovingian king, Childeric III. He was most probably born on 2 April 748, barely two years before Pippin seized power by deposing Childeric and forcing him into exile in a monastery. Einhard's account of the last Merovingians has become classic: we must recognize that it is written with hindsight to justify Pippin's actions. The young Charles was the leader of the party which rode out some 150 kilometres to meet and escort Pope Stephen II when he arrived in the Frankish kingdom in the winter of 753 to crown Pippin. Seeking Pippin's support against the northern Italian kingdom of the Lombards, who were invading papal territory, Stephen anointed Pippin, Charles and his brother Carloman as kings and gave them the title 'Patrician of the Romans'. Pippin invaded Italy and laid siege to the Lombard capital of Pavia in 755, securing the papal territory from the Lombards, who had besieged Rome. It was this alliance with the papacy which helped to establish and to define the new Carolingian dynasty.

On 24 September 768 Pippin died and Charlemagne and his younger brother Carloman succeeded their father as joint kings. Charles inherited the outer parts of the kingdom, bordering on the sea, namely Neustria, western Aquitaine, and the northern parts of Austrasia, while Carloman retained the inner parts: southern Austrasia, Septimania, eastern Aquitaine, Burgundy, Provence and Swabia, lands bordering on Italy. For the first thirty years of Charlemagne's reign military expeditions were almost an annual event, for war after a spring assembly and the subsequent distribution of plunder was a crucial element of Carolingian rule. Loyal followers were rewarded with 'gold and silver and silks and other gifts', in the words of the Annals of Lorsch for 793.

There were normally two assemblies each year: one a general one and the other attended only by the most important men in the kingdom and the king's chief advisers. At the annual assembly gifts were generally exchanged, disputes between members of the political community resolved and ambassadors received. From 779 we have ordinances from his assemblies, known as capitularies. Charlemagne controlled the territories over which he ruled by sending out *missi dominici*, royal agents (normally a cleric and a noble) charged with making regular circuits through specifically defined territorial entities to announce the king's will, to gather information on the perform- ance of local officials, and to execute justice and correct abuses. In 802 Charlemagne ordered that all his subjects over 12 years of age should swear a new oath of fidelity to him as emperor, not to harm the honour of the realm. Charlemagne's central administration depended on his palace chapel, a staff of clerics who drew up the documents of his reign. His capitularies, drawn up after the assemblies, were copied and circulated by the clerks of the palace chapel. In 792/4 weights, measures and coinage were reformed.

We know of the principal events of Charlemagne's reign from several sets of annals, which describe what happened in the kingdom year by year. The most important and most detailed are the Royal Frankish Annals, a Latin text compiled in stages and copied across his empire. After defeating a revolt in Aquitaine, where his father had fought dukes asserting their independence from the Franks, Charlemagne married the daughter of the Lombard king Desiderius. He inherited his

brother's territories after Carloman's sudden death in December 771. In 773 he abandoned his wife and invaded the Lombard kingdom, where Carloman's widow Gerberga had fled
with her children. In June 774 he captured Pavia, deposed
Desiderius and captured their treasure, proclaiming himself
king of the Lombards. He also went to Rome and renewed the
promise that his father had made to the pope, placing a copy
of the document on St Peter's tomb.

In 778 Charlemagne entered Spain; hoping to attack the emir
of Cordova, but he abandoned the siege of Saragossa and on
his return his army was ambushed by Basques in the Pyrenees,
a defeat which became known as the Battle of Roncevaux and
was celebrated in the old French epic, *The Song of Roland*. In
781 Charles made his oldest three sons kings under his rule.
The eldest, Charles, received the kingdom of Neustria, containing the regions of Anjou, Maine and Touraine. The second
eldest, Pippin, was made king of Italy. His third son, Louis,
became king of Aquitaine.

Throughout most of his reign he fought the pagan Saxons,
who had repeatedly raided his father's kingdom. In 772 he
captured the treasure deposited at the Saxon shrine of the
Irminsul and marched to the River Weser. Raids and counter-
attacks took place almost every year: in 778 the Saxons sacked
settlements on the right bank of the Rhine. In 782, after a Saxon
rebellion in which four Frankish counts and twenty other nobles
were killed, Charlemagne in revenge beheaded 4,500 Saxons.
He was concerned to evangelize Saxony and in 785 he forced
Christian baptism on the Saxon leader Duke Widukind and his
people, and set up bishoprics in the new territories. From 794
thousands of Saxons were deported from their homeland in a
bid to break down Saxon power, and peace was finally made
in 803.

The duchy of Bavaria had been subject to the Merovingians
and the young Duke Tassilo had fought with Charlemagne's
father Pippin against the Lombards. In 788 Charlemagne
deposed Tassilo, who was accused of having deserted during
Pippin's campaign against Aquitaine, and annexed Bavaria to
become a part of his realm. There were serious rebellions in

Bavaria and Saxony in 792–3. From 791 to 796 Carolingian
armies fought the Avars, the dominant force in central Europe
for over two hundred years and a military threat to the eastern
frontier of Frankish territory. The great Avar treasure was
brought back to Aachen in 796 and an Anglo-Saxon annal
records that it filled fifteen oxcarts.

The Frankish Church took a distinctive stand on dogma,
and Charlemagne saw the protection of the Church and the
condemnation of heresy as a part of his mission. At the Synod
of Frankfurt in 794 an assembly of bishops from Francia, Italy
and Germany condemned Adoptionism, the teaching on the
Trinity of the Spanish bishops Elipand of Toledo and Felix of
Urgel. In 799 at the Council of Aachen Felix recanted, after a
public debate with the Anglo-Saxon scholar Alcuin. At the same
time Frankish theologians condemned the Byzantine position
on the worship due to images of Christ, the Virgin Mary and
the saints, 'so that the enemy advancing from the east may be
struck helpless by the judgement of the holy fathers in the
western lands given us by God's grace': Charlemagne's approving comments on the Frankish treatise against the Greeks are
preserved in the margins of the earliest copy.

After an attack on Pope Leo III at Rome in April 799 Leo
crossed the Alps and met Charlemagne at Paderborn, and
Charles went to Rome to clear his name. He presided over an
assembly which heard the complaints against the pope. In the
words of the Annals of Lorsch,

> since the title of emperor had become extinct among the Greeks
> and a woman [Empress Irene] claimed the imperial authority, it
> seemed to Pope Leo and to all the holy fathers who were present
> at the council and to the rest of the Christian people that Charles,
> king of the Franks, ought to be named emperor, for he held Rome
> itself where the Caesars were always accustomed to reside and
> also other cities in Italy, Gaul and Germany. Since almighty God
> had put all these places in his power it seemed fitting to them
> that, with the help of God, and in accordance with the request
> of all the Christian people, he should hold this title.

On Christmas day 800, in the basilica of St Peter's, Charlemagne was crowned emperor by Pope Leo III. The new title reflected his rule over many peoples. The imperial coronation created tension with the Byzantine emperors, but in 812 the Byzantine emperor Michael acknowledged Charlemagne as a brother and a king.

In 810 and 811 Charlemagne organized coastal and military defences against the Northmen. Had it not been for the murder of Godfrid king of the Danes in 810, he might have had to face a serious attack on his empire, for Godfrid had assembled an army, claimed to have subdued Frisia and Saxony and boasted that he would come to Aachen. But his successor made peace. In 806 Charlemagne drew up a division of his territories between his three sons after his death, and sought to establish their mutual cooperation, but the deaths of Charles and Pippin rendered this void. The division made no mention of the imperial title. In 813 Charlemagne crowned his son Louis as emperor at Aachen. He died on 28 January 814.

In ruling an empire which covered some 1,200,000 square kilometres Charlemagne saw the advancement of learning as a part of his task. His court was a centre for foreign scholars, and he himself discussed biblical and secular learning, and sought information about astronomy. Alcuin's handbook on rhetoric and the virtues is cast in the form of a dialogue between Alcuin and Charlemagne and his palace school was a centre to which intelligent young men like Einhard were sent. His children were instructed in the liberal arts. This learning served to advance the understanding of the divine law of which the king was the agent. His capitularies show a careful study of canon law. From 794 his itinerant court settled in the palace at Aachen, where the magnificent octagonal chapel, which survives to this day, was constructed with columns brought from Rome and Ravenna. The Latin poetry composed at his court praises Charlemagne in Virgilian terms, as a patron of the arts, ruling in a new Athens, and as the father of Europe. Charlemagne had welcomed scholars from all over Europe to his court.

Explicitly following the example of Josiah, the Old Testament king of the Israelites who had called his people back to God, Charlemagne sought to instruct his people. The main work of the Carolingian renaissance was to restore Latin to its position as a literary language, and to reintroduce a correct system of spelling and an improved handwriting. There was a programmatic attempt to ensure that the Church followed the rite of the see of Rome. Every bishop was required to set up a school in his diocese and priests were to instruct their congregation about the basics tenets of Christianity. A sermon collection, prepared for Charlemagne by Paul the Deacon, was to be used throughout the empire. Monks and nuns were to obey their monastic rules. The laws of the separate peoples within the empire were reformed. In May 813 Church councils were held at Tours, Arles, Reims, Chalons and Mainz to give answers to questions about how Christians should lead their lives, pray for the emperor, learn the creed and the Lord's Prayer, how monks should follow the Rule of St Benedict. The emperor was concerned with the way of life and the salvation of his subjects.

Einhard describes Charlemagne's death from a sudden fever: Bishop Thegan, who wrote a biography of Charlemagne's successor Louis the Pious, described him on his deathbed correcting the Latin version of the Gospels with the help of learned Greeks and Syrians, summoning Archbishop Hildebold of Cologne to give him the last sacrament and then making the sign of the cross and singing a Psalm verse: 'Into thy hands O Lord I commend my spirit' (Psalm 31: 5).

Chronology

748 Birth of Charlemagne.
768 24 September: death of Pippin III; 9 October: coronation of Charlemagne and Carloman in Noyon.
769 War in Aquitaine.
771 4 December: death of Carloman.
c. 771 Birth of Einhard.
772 Start of Saxon wars. Destruction of the Irminsul shrine.
773 Invasion of the Lombard kingdom.
774 Siege of Pavia; capture of King Desiderius.
777 Mass baptism of Saxons.
778 15 August: defeat of Charlemagne's army at Roncevalles.
783 Battle at the River Hase.
783 Death of Queen Hildegard.
785 Hardrad's conspiracy against Charlemagne.
787 Charlemagne goes to Rome; surrender of the duke of Benevento.
788 Deposition of Duke Tassilo of Bavaria.
792 Rebellion of Pippin the Hunchback.
793 Campaign against the Avars.
794 Death of Queen Fastrada.
795 Death of Pope Hadrian.
796 Defeat of the Avars.
799 Attack on Pope Leo III and his flight to Paderborn.
800 Imperial coronation of Charlemagne.
802 Arrival of the elephant Abul Abaz.
806 Einhard takes the *Divisio Regnorum* to Rome.

810 Death of Godfrid, King of the Danes. Death of Charlemagne's sister Gisela, abbess of Chelles. Death of Pippin, king of Italy.

811 Death of Charles, son of Charlemagne.

812 Charlemagne recognized as Basileus and Imperator by the Byzantine emperors.

813 Destruction of the bridge at Mainz. September: coronation of Louis the Pious at Aachen. Einhard invites Charlemagne to make Louis his heir.

814 28 January: death of Charlemagne.

815 11 January: Louis the Pious grants an estate at Michelstadt to Einhard.

823 13 June: birth of Charles the Bald.

827 Einhard sends to Rome for the bodies of Marcellinus and Peter.

828 Easter: arrival of the relics of Marcellinus and Peter at Aachen. November: transfer of the relics to Seligenstadt.

830 Rebellion of Lothar against Louis the Pious.

833 13 November: deposition of Louis the Pious.

834 1 March: restoration of Louis the Pious.

840 14 March: death of Einhard. 20 June: death of Louis the Pious.

c. 840 Birth of Notker.

883 Visit of Charles the Fat to St Gall.

884 Notker's *Liber Ymnorum*.

887 Deposition of Charles the Fat.

912 6 April: death of Notker.

Further Reading

EINHARD

Becher, Mathias, *Charlemagne* (New Haven, 2003).

Collins, Roger, *Charlemagne* (London, 1998).

Dutton, Paul Edward, *Charlemagne's Courtier: The Complete Einhard* (Peterborough, Ont., 1998).

——, *Charlemagne's Mustache and Other Cultural Clusters of a Dark Age* (Basingstoke, 2004).

Ganshof, François Louis, 'Einhard, Biographer of Charlemagne', in Ganshof, *The Carolingians and the Frankish Monarchy: Studies in Carolingian History* (Ithaca, NY, 1971), pp. 1–16.

Ganz, David, *Einhard* (Manchester, 2008).

——, 'Einhard's Charlemagne: The Characterization of Greatness', in J. Story (ed.), *Charlemagne: Empire and Society* (Manchester, 2005), pp. 38–51.

——, 'Einhardus Peccator', in C. P. Wormald and J. Nelson (eds.), *Lay Intellectuals in the Carolingian World* (Cambridge, 2007), pp. 37–50.

Hauck, Karl (ed.), *Das Einhardkreuz: Vorträge und Studien der Münsteraner Diskussion zum arcus Einhardi* (Göttingen, 1974).

Hellmann, Siegmund, 'Einhards literarische Stellung', in Helmut Beumann (ed.), *Ausgewählte Abhandlungen zur Historiographie und Geistesgeschichte des Mittelalters* (Darmstadt, 1961), pp. 159–229.

Kempshall, Matthew, 'Some Ciceronian Models for Einhard's Life of Charlemagne', *Viator*, 26 (1995), pp. 11–37.

King, P. D., *Charlemagne: Translated Sources* (Kendal, 1987). This includes translations of the Royal Frankish Annals, the Revised Royal Frankish Annals and the Astronomer's Life of the Emperor Louis as well as several important capitularies.

Lowe, Heinz, 'Die Entstehungszeit der Vita Karoli Einhards', *Deutsches Archiv*, 39 (1983), pp. 85–103.

Smith, Julia, 'Einhard: The Sinner and the Saints', *Transactions of the Royal Historical Society*, 6th Series 13 (2003), pp. 55–77.

Tischler, Mathias M., *Einharts Vita Karoli: Studien zur Entstehung, Überlieferung und Rezeption* (Hanover, 2001).

NOTKER

Ganz, David, 'Humour as History in Notker's Gesta Karoli Magni', in E. King, J. Schaefer and W. Wadley (eds.), *Monks, Nuns and Friars in Medieval Society* (Sewanee, Tenn., 1989), pp. 171–83.

Goetz, Hans-Werner, *Strukturen der spätkarolingischen Epoche im Spiegel der Vorstellungen eines zeitgenössichen Mönchs: Ein Interpretation der Gesta Karoli Notkers von Sankt Gallen* (Bonn, 1981).

Goldberg, Eric, ' "More Devoted to the Equipment of Battle than the Splendor of Banquets": Frontier Kingship, Martial Ritual, and Early Knighthood at the Court of Louis the German', *Viator*, 30 (1999), pp. 1–78.

Haefele, Hans-Frider, 'Studien zu Notkers Gesta Karoli', *Deutsches Archiv*, 15 (1959), pp. 358–93.

Halphen, Louis, *Études critiques sur l'histoire de Charlemagne* (Paris, 1921).

Hartmann, Wilfried, *Ludwig der Deutsche* (Darmstadt, 2002).

Hiley, David, 'Notker', in L. Macey (ed.), *Grove Music Online*.

Innes, Matthew, 'Memory, Orality and Literacy in an Early Medieval Society', *Past and Present*, 158 (1998), pp. 3–36.

Kershaw, Paul, 'Laughter after Babel's Fall: Misunderstanding and Miscommunication in the Ninth-Century West', in Guy Halsall (ed.), *Humour, History and Politics in Late Antiquity and the Early Middle Ages* (Cambridge 2002), pp. 179–201.

Löwe, Heinz, 'Das Karlsbuch Notkers von St Gallen und sein zeitgeschichtlicher Hintergrund', reprinted in Löwe, *Von Cassiodor zu Dante* (Berlin, 1973), pp. 123–48.

MacLean, Simon, *Kingship and Politics in the Late Ninth Century: Charles the Fat and the End of the Carolingian Empire* (Cambridge, 2003).

Paris, Gaston, *Histoire poetique de Charlemagne* (1865).

Rankin, Susan, 'Ego itaque Notker scripsi', *Revue bénédictine*, 101 (1991), pp. 268–98.

Siegrist, Theodor, *Herrscherbild und Weltsicht bei Notker Balbulus: Untersuchungen zu den Gesta Karoli* (Zurich, 1963).

von den Steinen, Wolfram, *Notker der Dichter und seine geistige Welt*, 2 vols. (Berne, 1948).

Family tree and map

The Family of Charlemagne

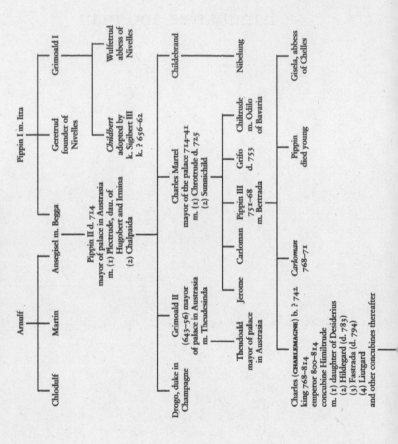

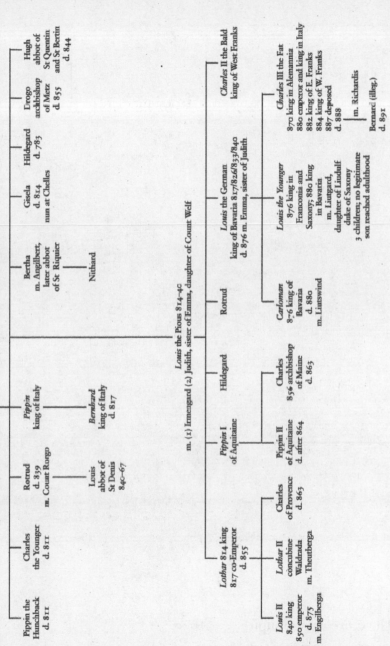

Pippin the Hunchback
d. 811

Charles the Younger
d. 811

Rotrud
d. 839
m. Count Rorgo

Louis
abbot of St Denis
840-67

Pippin
king of Italy

Bernard
king of Italy
d. 817

Bertha
m. Angilbert, later abbot of St Riquier

Nithard

Gisela
d. 814
nun at Chelles

Hildegard
d. 783

Drogo
archbishop of Metz
d. 855

Hugh
abbot of St Quentin and St Bertin
d. 844

Louis the Pious 814-40
m. (1) Irmengard (2) Judith, sister of Emma, daughter of Count Welf

Lothar 814 king
817 co-Emperor
d. 855

Pippin I
of Aquitaine

Hildegard

Rotrud

Louis the German
king of Bavaria 817/826/833/840
d. 876 m. Emma, sister of Judith

Charles II the Bald
king of West Franks

Louis II king
850 emperor
d. 875
m. Engelberga

Lothar II
concubine Waldrada
m. Theutberga

Charles
of Provence
d. 863

Pippin II
of Aquitaine
d. after 864

Charles
856 archbishop of Mainz
d. 863

Carloman
8~6 king of Bavaria
d. 880
m. Liutswind

Louis the Younger
876 king in Franconia and Saxony, 880 king in Bavaria
m. Liutgard, daughter of Liudulf duke of Saxony
3 children; no legitimate son reached adulthood

Charles III the Fat
8~70 king in Alemannia
880 emperor and king in Italy
882 king of E. Franks
884 king of W. Franks
887 deposed
d. 888
m. Richardis

Bernard (illeg.)
d. 891

Note: Names in italics are of kings

York

R. Rhine
Konstanz
THURGAU
Lake Constance

Zurich
R. Thur
St Gall

ENGLAND

London

Canterbury

FRIS

R. Waal
Nimegen

Ghent
Maastricht
Aachen
Liège

Amiens
Rouen
Soissons
R. Seine
Chelles
Rheims
Metz
Paris
Châlons
R. Moselle

BRITTANY
Rennes
NEUSTRIA

Sens

Orleans
Tours

Bourges
R. Loire
BURGUNDY
Besançon

Poitiers

AQUITAINE

R. Saône

Clermont
Lyons
Vienne
Grenoble

PROVENCE

Bordeaux

GASCONY
R. Garonne

R. Rhône

ASTURIAS

Toulouse
Avignon
Arles

Carcassonne
Narbonne

NAVARRE
SEPTIMANIA
R. Berre

R. Ebro

Saragossa

0
200 miles
0
200 kilometres

The Carolingian Empire
Tortosa

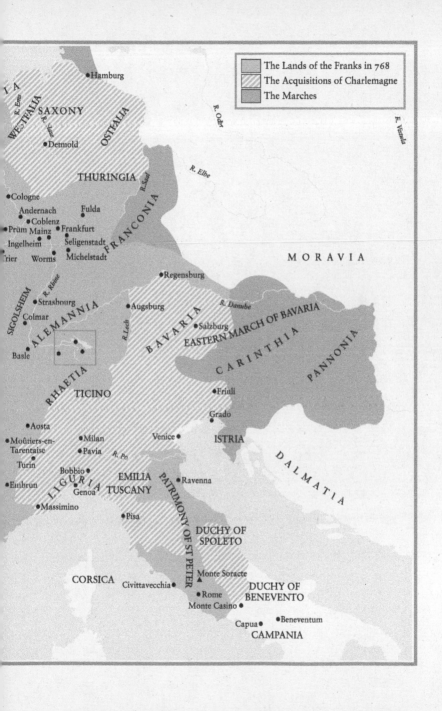

The Lands of the Franks in 768
The Acquisitions of Charlemagne
The Marches

R. Ems

WESTFALIA

R. Eder

SAXONY

OSTFALIA

•Hamburg

R. Oder

F. Vistula

•Detmold

THURINGIA

R. Elbe

R. Saal

•Cologne

Andernach

•Coblenz

Fulda•

FRANCONIA

•Prüm Mainz

•Frankfurt

Ingelheim

Seligenstadt

Trier

Worms

Michelstadt

MORAVIA

SIGOLSHEIM

R. Rhine

•Strasbourg

Colmar

ALEMANNIA

RHAETIA

Basle

•Regensburg

•Augsburg

R. Lech

BAVARIA

•Salzburg

R. Danube

EASTERN MARCH OF BAVARIA

CARINTHIA

PANNONIA

TICINO

•Friuli

Grado

•Aosta

•Moûtiers-en-Tarentaise

Turin

•Milan

•Pavia

R. Po

Venice•

ISTRIA

DALMATIA

Bobbio•

LIGURIA

Genoa•

EMILIA

TUSCANY

•Embrun

•Massimino

Ravenna•

PATRIMONY OF ST PETER

•Pisa

DUCHY OF
SPOLETO

CORSICA

Civittavecchia•

Monte Soracte▲

•Rome

Monte Casino

DUCHY OF
BENEVENTO

Capua•

•Beneventum

CAMPANIA

EINHARD

THE LIFE OF CHARLEMAGNE

Introduction

We know little about Einhard's life, though we know more about him than about most of his contemporaries. This is because we have several different sorts of sources for his life: in addition to the Life of Charlemagne translated here, there is his own account of how his agents removed the relics of the Roman martyrs Marcellinus and Peter from the catacombs and brought them to his church at Michelstadt (and then to Seligenstadt), and of the various miracles they performed there,[1] there is a collection of letters assembled at his monastery of St Bavo in Ghent, there are charters (one of which may have his own autograph signature) and there is a drawing of his arch-shaped reliquary; a moving letter preserved by Lupus of Ferrières, to whom it was written, tells of his grief at the death of his wife Imma; and Einhard is mentioned in a number of other contemporary texts. All these references have been helpfully collected, and expertly translated, by Paul Dutton in his book *Charlemagne's Courtier: The Complete Einhard*.

From the preface to Einhard's Life of Charlemagne, composed by Walahfrid Strabo soon after 840 and translated on page 15, we know that Einhard was born to a wealthy family living in the valley of the Main which flows into the Rhine close to Mainz, in the eastern part of the kingdom of the Franks. He was born soon after 770 and was given his father's name. The family sent him as a boy to the great monastery of Fulda, where he was educated, and made a grant to the abbey of land which they held in the Maingau. In the 790s he was sent by the abbot to Charlemagne's court, where he became the pupil of the Yorkshireman Alcuin who had gone to teach there, and succeeded him as teacher at the palace school. In the court poetry of 796 by Alcuin and the learned Visigothic poet Theodulph, Einhard is mentioned as an honoured member of the circle of intellectuals and is teased about his height but admired for his energy. He is described as a poet and a learned man, able to explain problems of grammar and arithmetic. This is a tribute to his talents, for he was markedly younger than most of the members of that circle. Alcuin, in a letter written to Charlemagne in 799, regarded Einhard as a pupil, a *fidelis* of the emperor and an expert in rhetoric and mathematical figures, and he wrote a poem for his Aachen house.

He himself wrote in the preface to the Life of Charlemagne of 'the constant friendship with [Charlemagne] and his children after I began living at his court'. Early in 806 he was chosen to take the details of the *Divisio Regnorum*, Charlemagne's plan for the division of his kingdoms after his death, to Pope Leo III for his signature. In 813 he was chosen to ask Charlemagne to crown his son Louis as his successor at an assembly in Aachen. After Charlemagne's death he was rewarded with the abbacies of the monasteries of St Peter and St Bavo at Ghent, St Servatius at Maastricht, and St Wandrille on the River Seine. On 11 February 815 he and his wife were granted a large estate at Michelstadt in the Odenwald, with a wooden church, fourteen serfs with their wives and children, and forty dependents. He wrote official letters for Louis and may also have drafted imperial legislation. In 827–8 Einhard procured relics of Sts Marcellinus and Peter from Rome for his church at Seligenstadt, and wrote a full account of how they were brought to Germany and the miracles they performed. Letters he wrote between 825 and 840 have survived, revealing his role as a courtier and in the complicated politics of the rebellions against Louis. A poem by Walahfrid Strabo describing Easter at Louis's court in 829 mentions Einhard as a prominent courtier and praises his unmatched gifts. We have a collection of 65 letters assembled at St Bavo's in Ghent, in which Einhard wrote to the emperor and his sons Lothar and Louis the German, to bishops and counts, but also to his deputies concerning the collection of revenues, the slaughter of cattle and the supply of wax. The death of his wife Emma in January 836 provoked a remarkable exchange of letters revealing his grief. He died on 14 March 840. His epitaph, composed by Hrabanus Maurus, the abbot of Fulda, praised him as prudent, wise and eloquent and skilful in the art of many things.

This sketch of Einhard's career makes it clear that we are dealing with an insider, a prominent courtier, whose wisdom and intelligence were admired by contemporaries. His status gives him a particular authority as the biographer of Charlemagne. He tells us why he felt he needed to write the book: he had been nourished by the emperor, he felt that no one could imitate his deeds and he feared that his greatness would be forgotten. He sets the *Vita Karoli* in a world of praise of the ruler, and it is helpful to see his work in this tradition. Praise was a proper concern of ancient orators; Cicero explained what topics were to be considered in praising people:

> The attributes of persons are name, nature, manner of life, fortune, habit, feeling, interests, purposes, achievements, accidents, speeches. Nature considered as to sex, race, place of birth, family, what are one's ancestors or kin, age, advantages given to mind or body by nature, as for example, whether one is strong or weak, tall or short, handsome or ugly, swift or slow, bright or dull, retentive or forgetful, affable or unmannerly, modest, patient or the contrary. (*De inventione* 1.24.34)

In order to write his biography of Charlemagne Einhard had to discuss the early life of his hero.

Einhard's Life of Charlemagne was one of the most popular medieval Latin texts, surviving in over 123 manuscripts and frequently printed, and it has shaped our picture of Charlemagne. The originality of the life was recognized by contemporaries. It rapidly became a school text, presented by Einhard's friend the court librarian Gerward to Louis the Pious with the following verse preface: 'Gerward the humble servant wrote these verses in your praise and your eternal memory, great prince, who with a kindly mind raised your famous name to the stars. Know, prudent reader, that magnificent Einhard wrote this *gesta* of great Charles.' The Carolingian poet and theologian Gottschalk read it at Fulda and noted the word used by Einhard to characterize the talkative Charlemagne (*dicaculus*).[2] Lupus of Ferrières quotes from it in the prologue to the Life of St Wigbert.[3] The *Gesta Abbatum Fontanellensium*, composed between 838 and 840, borrows from it.[4] It was known to Asser when he wrote his life of King Alfred.[5]

It is hard for a modern reader to recapture the originality of Einhard's work. In the preface to his Life of St Martin of Tours, Sulpicius Severus attacked secular biography:

Most men, being vainly devoted to the pursuit of worldly glory, have, as they imagined, acquired a memorial of their own names from this source, devoting their pens to the embellishment of the lives of famous men. This course, although it did not secure for them a lasting reputation, still has undoubtedly brought them some fulfilment of the hope they cherished. I have done so, both by preserving their own memory, though to no purpose, and because, through their having presented to the world the examples of great men, no small emulation has been excited in the bosoms of their readers. Yet, notwithstanding these things, their labours have in no degree borne upon the blessed and never-ending life to which we look forward. For what has a glory, destined to perish with the world, profited those men who have written on mere secular matters? Or what benefit has posterity derived from reading of Hector as a warrior, or Socrates as an expounder of philosophy? There can be no profit in such things, since it is not only folly to imitate the persons referred to, but absolute madness not to assail them with the utmost severity. For, in truth, those persons who estimate human life only by present actions have consigned their hopes to fables and their souls to the tomb. In fact, they gave themselves up to be perpetuated simply in the memory of mortals, whereas it is the duty of man rather to seek after eternal life than an eternal memorial and that, not by writing or fighting, or philosophizing, but by living a pious, holy and religious life.

So the idea that anyone other than a saint might deserve a biography was entirely new. Einhard tells us that he wrote about Charlemagne because his great deeds could scarcely be imitated, and his remarkable preface explains how 'the most famous and greatest of men' deserves a fitting literary commemoration. This programme of Ciceronian eloquence in the praise of rulers was in opposition to a Christian tradition which spurned such eloquence, preferring the simplicity of the apostles. It also opposed those who thought the deeds of the present inferior to those of the past. His sense of greatness could not be simply Christian.

The Carolingians recorded their history in annals, records of the chief events of each year, of which the most detailed and influential were the Royal Frankish Annals, most probably composed at the court. Einhard used this for his treatment of the reign of Charlemagne's father, Pippin, and for Charlemagne's early wars.[6] He also consulted documents in the royal archives, the *History of the Bishops of Metz* by Paul the Deacon, and most important, the Lives of the Caesars by Suetonius. Alcuin explained that for contemporaries to attain the authority of the ancients they had to read their works and memorize their phrases, and this is clearly what Einhard did with Suetonius. To commemorate his friend and master he chose to adapt the biographical schema of Suetonius' Lives. Suetonius provided the structure for Einhard's Life, offering an example of a biography which did not supply a chronological narrative, but tackled different topics in order. In addition, Suetonius provided information about the private life of the Caesars, so supplementing the narrative with features which conveyed the characteristic behaviour of the subject. The description of the ruler's birth, infancy, wars, public works and generosity in giving gifts, his navy, his marriages and children, his concern for his mother, how the children were raised, his reaction to their deaths, his friendships, the conspiracies against him, his appearance, his dress, his meals, his eloquence, his studies, the portents of his death and his will can all be found in the Life of Augustus and in many of Suetonius' Lives. The vocabulary is taken over directly, Suetonius supplying the turns of phrase and

combinations of words: Einhard followed him not only in the
range of topics he covered, but also in the terminology he used.
Although some of these phrases may well have been standard
usage, and may not derive directly from Suetonius, there are so
many of them that Einhard must have studied Suetonius' text
with care. The terminology for Charlemagne's private life, his
friendships, his appearance, his taste in food, his concern for
the liberal arts and the prodigies which presaged his death is
that of Suetonius, and there is no other obvious source.

This suggests that in his recollections of Charlemagne Einhard was searching for those features which could be matched
in the accounts of the twelve Caesars, and that he believed that
these features helped to secure Charlemagne's standing as the
greatest ruler of his age. He tells us that he will 'first write about
his deeds inside and outside the kingdom, then his way of life
and his pursuits, and finally his administration of the kingdom
and his death'. But the prime agent of historical explanation in
the *Vita Karoli* is Einhard's elaborate terminology of personal-
ity. Alcuin had said that an orator may secure the benevolence
of his audience if he describes the acts of his protagonists as
done bravely, wisely and with moderation. Einhard uses nouns
rather than adverbs: Charlemagne's acts arise from his greatness of soul, his discernment, his patience in adversity and his
constancy. Classical and Christian virtues have their place in
a public sphere which thus became a theatre for individual
greatness. But if we follow Einhard's Latin phrases back to
their sources we can find other echoes. This is not the place for
a full treatment, but it is worth noting that when Einhard speaks
of the wiser council of the Gascon duke Lupus, he uses a phrase
saniore consilio, which the Rule of St Benedict uses to describe
the behaviour of the abbot. At Fulda he would have heard the
Rule read aloud day by day. And he recalled it again when he
wrote that Charlemagne's treaty with the Byzantine emperors
avoided any source of trouble, just as the monks were to avoid
any inducement to sin (the Latin word *scandalum* is the same
in the Rule as in the Life).

Einhard may have had personal knowledge of Saxon campaigns: their invasions had crossed his ancestral estates, and he

would have learned, at court, of the campaigns of 794, 795 and 797. Because we can find facts in the Royal Frankish Annals we need not assume that Einhard could not remember them. There is even the possibility that he was involved in the composition of the Annals themselves. Einhard presents the Merovingians as unworthy to rule, echoing the treatment found in the *Annales Mettenses Priores* and he suggests that the mayors of the palace had attained a hereditary status. For Einhard, legitimate rule is related to power and the control of wealth.

There is much that we do not know about Einhard. Did he have older or younger siblings? Was he really the dwarf he is teased for being, and did that mean that he was unable to be a warrior? How much of a wrench was it for him to leave his family for the monastery, and did he regard Charlemagne as a substitute for his own father? What sort of a poet was he, and how important was that gift of creativity to him? What does it mean that he calls himself a sinner?[7] What role did his wife play, and did he share Lupus' views on the inferiority of women? Did they have any children? But we can answer some of the questions about his writings, and we can still visit the churches he built, admire the arch reliquary he designed and enjoy his literary skills.

There has been much discussion of when Einhard composed his Life. In an age of print a book can be read in many copies at the same time. In a manuscript culture copies circulated much more slowly. We can trace how the *Vita Karoli* spread from the different prefatory materials; the prose prologue in which he presented it to a friend, probably to be identified with Gerward, the librarian of the emperor Louis the Pious, and the verses in which Gerward identified Einhard as the author and presented a copy to Louis, the 'greatest prince'. Further evidence comes from texts which quote from Einhard's work. The *Vita Karoli* must have been written after the revolt of the Abrodites in 817, alluded to in the Life in chapter 12 where they are described as formerly allied with the Franks,[8] and probably after the collapse of the portico at Aachen in 817, referred to by Einhard as a portent of Charlemagne's death, but not otherwise mentioned as having occurred before 9 April 817.

Mathias Tischler has provided textual arguments suggesting that the phraseology of the *Vita Karoli* was used by Einhard in the *Translatio*, a work whose last miracle takes place on 28 August 830.[9] Thegan used it after 835, but before 837, in his biography of Louis the Pious.[10] By the time Notker read it and used it as the basis of his own book about Charlemagne it had become a standard text, studied by schoolboys as well as princes and widely quoted. Walahfrid Strabo, in his poem *De Imagine Tetrici* of 829 affirms: 'Happy the line that continues with such a grandson: grant Christ that he will follow in deeds whom he follows in name, in deed, in character, nature, life, virtue and triumphs, in peace, faith, piety, intellect, speech and dignity. In doctrine, judgement, result and in loyal offspring.'[11] In her biography of Charles the Bald, Janet Nelson suggests that 'from young Charles's earliest years Charlemagne was held up as a role-model for him'.[12] Einhard's Life made an excellent 'mirror' for a future ruler, and may well have been studied by Walahfrid and Charles in the mid-830s, soon after it was written.[13] Throughout his life Charles the Bald was compared to his more famous grandfather, about whom Einhard was the standard source for information. In 877 Charles himself quoted the *Vita Karoli* in a document he composed for Pope John VIII.[14] That Einhard composed the Life of Charlemagne in part to offer an account of his famous grandfather to the only one of Louis the Pious's children never to have met Charlemagne in person is a plausible reason why the work needed to be written, in addition to the powerful reasons which Einhard himself offers.

Einhard's Life of Charlemagne has survived in 123 manuscripts,[15] making it one of the most popular medieval Latin works. The earliest manuscripts of the *Vita Karoli* date from the second half of the ninth century: they can be divided into three versions. A, 'the official version', is characterized by having attached to it Einhard's preface, which does not name the author but identifies him as one who had received Charlemagne's *nutrimentum*, and including a mention of Roland as a victim of the battle at Roncevaux (778) in chapter 9.

The oldest manuscript of A, the 'Grimalt-Codex', Vatican Vat. Reg. Lat. 339, is 'the key witness' for the Carolingian text-history of the Life.[16] It was presented to Charlemagne's grandson Louis the German by the royal archchancellor Abbot Grimald of St Gall, probably in 867. The second recension, B, did not have Einhard's preface, or the mention of Roland, or the pelts of otters and ermines, but it did have a dedicatory verse by Gerward, the librarian of Louis the Pious, indicating Einhard, with approval, as the author of the Life.

For the B version, Vienna 473, a late-ninth-century west German manuscript, is a historical compendium made at St Amand which combines the Lives of the popes with a history of the Franks from Troy to the death of Dagobert in 662, a continuation to the death of Charles Martel in 741, the Royal Frankish Annals from 741 to 814 and portions of Einhard's text, followed by the Annals from 814 to 829 and a brief genealogy of the Arnulphings and a summary of Frankish history to 840.[17]

For the C version of the text the manuscripts are Paris BN Lat. 10758, copied for Hincmar of Reims after 877 at the end of a major collection of Frankish law texts; and Vatican Pal. 243, a late-ninth-century manuscript, copied in the region of St Amand, which came to Lorsch.

The standard edition of Einhard's Life was published in the Monumenta Germaniae Historica in 1911, and is the revision by O. Holder-Egger of the edition by G. H. Pertz first published in 1829. It divides the text according to the chapter divisions first used by F. Bessel in his Helmstadt edition of 1667 but includes the different chapters, and their titles, devised by Walahfrid Strabo (c. 809–49). Walahfrid, brought to the monastery of the Reichenau, was later sent to study at Fulda under Hrabanus Maurus. In 829 he came to the court of Louis the Pious and acted as one of the teachers of his youngest son, Charles the Bald. At the court he met Einhard. In 838 he was made abbot of the Reichenau, deposed in 840 but restored as abbot in 842. An accomplished poet from his youth, he wrote court poetry, versified saints' lives and an account of the death-bed vision of Abbot Wetti, who was escorted to the next world

and saw Charlemagne in hell. His chapter divisions are given
in the margins of this translation.

NOTES

1. *Furta Sacra: Thefts of Relics in the Central Middle Ages*, with a
    new preface by Patrick J. Geary (Princeton, 2003).
2. D. C. Lambot, *Œuvres théologiques et grammaticales de
    Godescalc d'Orbais*, Spicilegium Sacrum Lovaniense, Etudes de
    Documents, 30 (Louvain, 1945), p. 489.
3. 'tanti viri facta non mandata memoriae', Vita s. Wigberti Pro-
    logus, *Monumenta Germaniae Historica, Scriptores in Folio*, vol.
    XV, p. 38.
4. E. Tremp, *Studien zu den Gesta Hludovici imperatoris des Trierer
    Chorbischofs Thegan*, *Monumenta Germaniae Historica*,
    Schriften, 32 (Hanover, 1986), p. 38. M. Tischler, *Einharts Vita
    Karoli: Studien zur Entstehung, Überlieferung und Rezeption*,
    Monumenta Germaniae Historica Schriften, 48 (Hanover,
    2001), p. 125.
5. S. Keynes and M. Lapidge, *Alfred the Great*, Penguin Classics
    (Harmondsworth, 1983), p. 55.
6. The Royal Frankish Annals, and the revised version composed
    soon after Charlemagne's coronation, are most conveniently
    translated in P. D. King, *Charlemagne: Translated Sources*
    (Kendal, 1987). The best treatment of how Einhard used the
    Annals remains that of Halphen in his edition, *Eginhard: Vie de
    Charlemagne* (Paris, 1923; 3rd edn., 1938). See also G. Wolf,
    'Einige Beispiele für Einhards hofhistoriographischen Euphem-
    ismus', in H. Scheffers (ed.), *Einhard: Studien zu Leben und
    Werk* (Darmstadt, 1997), pp. 311–22.
7. Cf. David Ganz, 'Einhardus Peccator', in C. P. Wormald and
    J. Nelson (eds.), *Lay Intellectuals in the Carolingian World*
    (Cambridge, 2007), pp. 37–50.
8. *Abroditos, qui cum Francis olim foederati erant.*
9. Tischler, *Einharts Vita Karoli*, pp. 173–7.
10. Tremp, *Studien zu den Gesta Hludovici imperatoris*, pp. 57–60.
11. *De Imagine Tetrici* is edited in *Monumenta Germaniae Historica*,
    Poetae II. 375–6, and translated by M. W. Herren, 'The *De
    Imagine Tetrici* of Walahfrid Strabo: Edition and Translation',
    Journal of Medieval Latin, 1 (1991), pp. 118–39.

12. Janet Nelson, *Charles the Bald* (London, 1992), p. 84.
13. Charles's education has been much discussed, and often attributed to Walahfrid. In Ermoldus' poem the young Charles the Bald has a tutor and a poem by Walahfrid addresses a teacher at the palace named Thomas. Abbot Makward to Prüm is referred to several times as a teacher of Charles.
14. K. Eckhardt, 'Das Protokoll von Ravenna und die Kaiserkronung Karls des Kahlen', *Deutsches Archiv*, 23 (1967), 295–311, at p. 304.
15. Full descriptions of all manuscripts are found in Tischler, *Einharts Vita Karoli*, pp. 20–44. Note that the contemporary contents list on fo. 1ᵛ and the title on fo. 305r of Paris BNF latin 10756 identify the text as *ab einhardo dicata*.
16. Tischler, *Einharts Vita Karoli*, pp. 102–51.
17. H. Reimitz, 'Ein karolingisches Geschichtsbuch aus St. Amand: Der codex Vindobonensis palat. 473', in C. Egger and H. Weigl (eds.), *Text-Schrift-Codex: Quellenkundliche Arbeiten aus dem Institut fur Österreichische Geschichtsforschung* (Vienna, 2000), pp. 34–90, at pp. 38, 47–50.

WALAHFRID'S PREFACE

Einhard is known to have written the account of the life and deeds of the most glorious emperor Charles which follows. Among all the palace officials at that time he was esteemed with great praise, not only for his knowledge but also for the complete honesty of his way of life. Because he was present at most of these events he attested them with the purest truth.

He was born in Eastern Francia,[1] in a region called the Maingau. He received the rudiments of his education as a boy at the monastery of Fulda under the teacher of the martyr St Boniface. From there he was sent to the palace of Charles by Baugulf, the abbot of the monastery, not so much because of the nobility which was so clear in him as because of his particular capacity and intelligence, and the wisdom which later shone forth in him. Charles was the keenest of all kings to seek out and support wise men so that they might philosophize with all delight. Almost all of the kingdom entrusted to him by God was so foggy and almost blind, but he made it luminous with the new ray of knowledge, almost unknown to this barbarous land, with God lighting the way so it could see. But now studies are growing weak, and the light of wisdom because it is less loved grows rarer among most people.

So this little man (for his height seemed contemptible) grew so great in glory, prudence and goodness in the palace of Charles the lover of wisdom, that there was almost no one else among the many officials of the king's majesty to whom the king, the most powerful and the wisest man of that time, entrusted so many secrets. And in truth that was not undeserved, so that not only in the time of Charles but also, which

is far more wonderful, in the time of the emperor Louis, when
the republic of the Franks was battered by many different dis-
turbances, and was falling in many ways, with God's protection
Einhard defended it with a wonderful and divinely inspired
distance. So the height of his reputation, which attracted envy
from many, did not soon abandon him or set him among
dangers he could not escape. I tell you this so that there will be
little doubt about what he said, since he knows about the special
praise he recorded out of love of his protector and the truth he
wished to convey to the interested reader. I Strabo introduced
chapter titles and divisions into this little book where it seemed
fitting, so that someone searching for particular topics should
have an easier access to them.

THE LIFE OF
CHARLEMAGNE

After I decided to write about the life, character and no small part of the accomplishments of my lord and foster father, Charles, that most excellent and deservedly most famous king, I determined to do so with as much brevity as I could. I took pains to omit none of the facts that have come to my notice nor to irritate the minds of those who are critical by supplying at great length an account of everything new, if it is possible to avoid angering with a new work those who criticize the ancient monuments composed by the most learned and eloquent of men. And yet I do not doubt that there are many people, devoted to contemplation and learning, who think that the circumstances of the present age should not be so neglected that almost everything that happens now – not worthy of any memory – should be condemned to silence and oblivion. Some people are so led on by love of lasting fame that they would rather insert the famous deeds of others into any sort of writings than remove the fame of their own name from the memory of posterity by writing nothing.[1] But I did not see why I should refuse to undertake a composition of this sort, since I was aware that no one could write about these things more truthfully than I could. I was present and knew them by the witness of my own eyes, as they say,[2] and I could not know clearly whether they would be written about by anyone else.

I thought it would be better to write these things down, along with other things, which are well known for the memory of posterity, rather than to suffer the most famous life of this most excellent king, the greatest of all the men of his age, and his remarkable deeds which men of our own time can barely imitate, to be swallowed up in the shadows of oblivion. There is still another not unreasonable impulse, which would have sufficed on its own to compel me to write these things, namely, the nurture he bestowed on me and the perpetual friendship with him and his children after I began living at his court. Through this he so bound me to him and put me in his debt, both in life and death, that I would rightly seem and be judged ungrateful if I forgot the many kindnesses he bestowed on me and passed over in silence the most famous and illustrious deeds of a man who had deserved the best from me. Nor could I allow his life to remain without written memorial and proper praise, as if he had never lived. But to write and set forth such a life would need, not my little talent, which is poor and small and almost non-existent, but would tax the eloquence of a Cicero.

Here is the book for you,[3] containing an account of the most famous and greatest of men. In it there is nothing you should wonder at apart from his deeds, except perhaps that I, a barbarian, with too little training in the language of Rome,[4] should have thought I could write something correct or fitting in Latin, and rushed headlong into such great impudence that I might be thought to have despised the advice of Cicero, who in the first book of his *Tusculan Disputations*, when he speaks of Latin authors, says: 'For people to set their thoughts down in writing when they cannot organize or make them clear or charm their reader with any delight is an intemperate abuse of leisure and of letters.'[5] This opinion of the famous orator might have deterred me from writing, but I had resolved rather to risk the judgements of men, and to endanger my own feeble talent by writing, than to neglect the memory of so great a man for the sake of sparing myself.

c. I. About the Merovingians, who governed the Franks for a long time with the vain name of king

1. The family of the Merovingians, from which the Franks used to make their kings, is thought to have lasted until King Childeric, who was deposed and tonsured and forced into a monastery on the order of Pope Stephen.[6] Although it might seem to have ended with him, it had in fact been without

any strength for a long time and offered nothing of any worth except the empty name of king. For the wealth and power of the kingdom were in the possession of the governors of the palace, who were called mayors of the palace and the highest command in the kingdom belonged to them. The king's sole remaining function was to sit back on his throne with flowing hair,[7] his beard uncut, satisfied with the name of king and the appearance of ruling. He listened to ambassadors, wherever they came from, and when they departed he gave them replies which he had been taught or ordered to say. Except for the empty name of king and a small stipend which the prefect of the court granted as it seemed best, he owned nothing else of his own but one estate, and that with a small income. There he had a house and servants ministering to his needs and showing obedience, but they were few in number. When he needed to travel he went in a cart pulled by yoked oxen and was led by a cowherd in the country manner. Thus he went to the palace and also to the public assembly of his people, which was held every year for the welfare of the kingdom, and thus he used to return home. But the administration of the kingdom and everything which was to be planned or executed at home or abroad was arranged by the prefect of the court.

2. When Childeric was deposed, Pippin, the father of King Charles, held that office, as if by hereditary right. For his father Charles[8] had brilliantly discharged that same civil office which had been laid down for him by his own father, Pippin. Charles overthrew the tyrants who claimed rule over all of Francia and so completely defeated the Saracens, who were attempting to occupy Gaul, in two great battles, one in Aquitaine at the city of Poitiers[9] and the second near Narbonne on the River Berre,[10] that he forced them to return to Spain. It was the custom of the people to give this honour only to those men who stood out above others because of the nobility of their birth and the extent of their wealth.

c. II. About Charles the mayor of the palace

Pippin, the father of King Charles, had held this office, which was left to him and to his brother Carloman by his grandfather and father, and they

c. III. About Pippin and Carloman, his sons

shared it in the greatest concord for a few years as if under that king mentioned above.[11] His brother Carloman – for reasons which are not clear, but it seems he was driven by a desire to lead a contemplative life – abandoned the heavy task of ruling an earthly kingdom and went to Rome in search of a quiet life and changed his style of life and was made a monk. With the brothers who had come there for this purpose he enjoyed for a few years the peace he had wished for in the monastery he built on Mount Soracte[12] near the church of St Sylvester. However, many nobles from Francia frequently visited Rome to carry out their vows and did not wish to miss seeing him who had once been their lord. They interrupted the peaceful life which he greatly loved by constantly greeting him and forced him to move. For when he saw that these frequent visits were interfering with his plan, he left Mount Soracte and retreated to the monastery of St Benedict located on Monte Cassino in the province of Samnium and spent what was left of his earthly life there in the religious life.[13]

c. IV. How Pippin was made king after Childeric and how long he ruled, and about his death and the division of the kingdom between his sons Charles and Carloman

3. Pippin, who had been mayor of the palace, was made king by the authority of the Roman pope and he ruled the Franks on his own for fifteen years or more. When the Aquitanian war which he waged against Waifar, duke of Aquitaine, for nine years,[14] was over, he died of oedema at Paris.[15] He was survived by his sons Charles and Carloman, to whom the succession fell by divine will. The Franks at a general assembly solemnly established both of them as kings on the condition that they should divide up the whole territory of the kingdom equally. Charles was to take up that part which their father Pippin had held and Carloman that part which their uncle Carloman had governed. Both of them agreed to these conditions and each received the part of the kingdom according to the manner agreed. That concord was kept, though with the greatest difficulty, since many on Carloman's side were trying to separate the agreement. Some went as far as plotting to turn them to war. But the outcome of things proved that the threat was more suspected

than real, and when Carloman died,[16] his wife and sons, with some who were the chiefs of his nobles, took refuge in Italy and for no reason at all, having rejected her husband's brother, his wife placed herself and her children under the protection of Desiderius, the king of the Lombards. Carloman had died from illness after they had ruled the kingdom for two years together, but Charles on his brother's death with the agreement of all of the Franks was made king.

4. I believe it would be senseless to write about his birth and infancy or even his childhood, since nothing was ever written down and there is no one still alive who claims to have knowledge of those things. Leaving aside what is unknown, I have decided to pass straight on to setting forth and explaining his deeds and way of life, and other aspects of his life. I shall first write about his deeds inside and outside the kingdom, then his way of life and his pursuits, and finally the administration of the kingdom and his death, leaving out nothing either worth knowing or necessary.

c. V. On the death of Carloman and Charles's beginnings

5. Of all the wars he waged he first took on the Aquitanian, which his father had begun but not finished, because he thought that it could be quickly accomplished. His brother was still alive and he asked for his help. And although his brother did not deliver the promised help he pursued the campaign he had begun with the greatest energy. He refused to abandon a war already in progress or to leave a task undone, until by determination and firmness he achieved the goal he had set himself. He forced Hunold, who had tried to occupy Aquitaine after the death of Waifar[17] and to renew a war almost over, to give up Aquitaine and seek refuge in Gascony.[18] But, unwilling to let him settle there, Charles crossed the River Garonne and through messengers commanded Lupus, the Gascon duke, to hand over the fugitive. If he did not do this swiftly, Charles would make war on him. Lupus gave way to wiser counsel and not only returned Hunold, but even entrusted himself and the province which he held to Charles's power.[19]

c. VI. How he ended the Aquitanian war

c. VII. How the war
against the Lombards
was undertaken and
completed

6. When things were settled in Aquitaine and that war ended, and after his co-ruler was taken from human affairs, at the request and on the prayers of Hadrian the bishop of the city of Rome he took up war against the Lombards.[20] This had been begun by his father at the request of Pope Stephen with great trouble, for some of the chief men of the Franks, whom he regularly consulted, were so opposed to his desire that they said openly that they would abandon the king and return home. Nevertheless war was taken up against King Aistulf and finished very quickly.[21] But although Charles and his father seem to have had a similar or rather the same reason for taking up war, it is agreed that the effort of fighting and the outcome were very different. For Pippin besieged Aistulf for a few days at Pavia and forced him both to surrender hostages and to restore the cities and castles seized from the Romans, and to swear an oath that he would not try to regain what he had returned. But after he had begun the war Charles did not stop until he had, by means of a long siege, worn out King Desiderius and accepted his surrender. He forced Desiderius' son Adalgis, in whom the hopes of all seemed to rest, to depart not only from the kingdom but also from Italy and to restore all that had been seized from the Romans.[22] He also defeated Rotgaud, the duke of Friuli,[23] who was plotting new opposition, and he brought all of Italy into his control and set up his son Pippin as king of what he had conquered.[24] I would relate here how difficult it was to enter Italy across the Alps and with what effort the Franks overcame the trackless mountain ridges, rocks thrust up to heaven and rugged peaks, were it not my intention in this work to record the manner of his life rather than the events of the wars which he waged. However, the end of this war was that Italy was conquered and King Desiderius sent into perpetual exile and his son Adalgis was driven out of Italy and the properties seized by the Lombard kings were restored to Hadrian, the ruler of the Roman Church.

c. VIII. Of the difficulty,
length and completion
of the Saxon war

7. After its end the Saxon war, which had seemed to have been interrupted, was begun again.[25] No war taken up by the Frankish people was ever longer, or more savage, or cost so much labour, because the Saxons, like almost all the peoples inhabiting Germany, were by nature fierce and given over to the worship of demons and were opposed to our religion and did not think it shameful to violate or transgress either human or divine laws. There were other reasons which could daily disturb the peace, for our boundaries and theirs almost always touched in open land, save for a few places where either vast forests or mountain ridges came between the lands of both of us and established a fixed boundary. Murders and thefts and fires did not cease in these regions. The Franks were so enraged by these things that they decided no longer to retaliate but to take up open war against them. So a war was taken up against them with great hostility on both sides and waged for thirty-three years without a break. But the losses of the Saxons were greater than those of the Franks. The war could have been ended faster if the faithlessness[26] of the Saxons had allowed it. It is hard to say how often they were conquered and surrendered humbly to the king and promised that they would do what was ordered, handed over the hostages demanded without delay and received the envoys who were sent. Sometimes they were so broken and weakened that they even promised to abandon the worship of demons and submit to the Christian religion. But although at times they were ready to do this, they were always so quick to break their promises, so that it is not possible to judge which of these can be said to have come to them more easily, for after the start of the war against them there was scarcely a year in which they did not make this sort of change. But the king's greatness of soul and perpetual firmness of mind, both in bad times and good, could not be conquered by their mutability or worn down by the task he had begun. For he never allowed those who did anything of this sort to go unpunished, but he himself would avenge their treachery and demand a fitting punishment until everyone who was accustomed to resist was crushed and brought back under his control either with an army he led himself or one sent under his counts. He moved ten thousand men who lived on both sides of the River Elbe,[27] with their wives and children, and dispersed them here and there throughout Gaul and Germany in many groups.[28] The war which had lasted for so many years ended on this condition imposed by the king and accepted by the Saxons, that they would reject the worship of demons and abandon their ancestral rites, and would take up the Christian faith and the sacraments of religion and, united with the Franks, would form one people with them.

c. IX. Of Charles's care and magnanimity
8. In this war, although it lasted for a long time, Charles met the enemy in battle no more than twice, once at a mountain called Osning in the place called Detmold, and again at the River Hase, and this happened in a month, with only a few days between them.[29] His enemies were destroyed and conquered in these two battles, so much so that they no longer dared to anger the king or to resist his coming, unless they were protected in some fortified place. In that war many of the nobility of the Franks and the Saxons who held high office were killed. At last, in the thirty-third year it ended, but in the meantime so many and such great wars in various regions had broken out against the Franks and had been governed by the king's skill that an observer might rightly doubt whether his patience or his success deserved more admiration. For the Saxon war began two years before the Italian and, though it was carried on without interruption, none of the wars which had to be fought elsewhere was abandoned or in any way postponed because of that equally burdensome struggle. For the king, who was the most outstanding of all the national leaders of his time for his prudence and his greatness of soul, did not abandon any war that had been begun or accomplished either because of the effort or the danger, but he learned to undergo and endure each according to its nature, nor was he accustomed to yield when in difficulties or to trust in good times to false smiling Fortune.[30]

c. X. What he did in Spain and about the disaster the Basques caused to his army
9. While he was vigorously and almost constantly pursuing the war with the Saxons, and had placed garrisons at suitable points along the frontier, he attacked Spain with as large a force as he could. After they had crossed the Pyrenees, he received the surrender of all the towns and fortified places he

came to. He was returning with his army safe and intact, apart from the fact that coming home, in the Pyrenean mountain range he had to experience a brief taste of the Basque treachery. For his army was advancing with a long baggage train, as the place and the narrow terrain required, and the Basques had set their ambush at the top of the mountain for, because of the density of the forests of which there are a great number, that is a spot most suitable for setting ambushes. They attacked the rear of the baggage train and drove the men of the rearguard and those who were marching in the rear down into the valley below. They joined battle with them and killed them to the last man, plundered the baggage and, protected by the night, went off in every direction as fast as they could. The Basques were aided by their light weapons and the place where this happened, while the Franks were disadvantaged both by the heaviness of their arms and the unevenness of the land.[31] In this battle, Eggihard, the overseer of the king's table,[32] Anselm, the count of the palace[33] and Roland, the prefect of the Breton March,[34] were killed, along with many others. This deed could not be avenged at that time, because the enemy had so dispersed that not even a rumour remained as to where they might be sought.

10. He also conquered the Bretons, who live on the shore of the ocean in the westernmost part of Gaul. Since they did not obey his commands he sent a force against them and compelled them to surrender hostages and promise that they would do as he ordered.[35] Afterwards he entered Italy with his army and journeyed by way of Rome to Capua, a city in Campania.[36] There he pitched camp and threatened the Beneventans with war unless they surrendered. Arichis, the leader of that people, sent his sons Rumold and Grimold with a great amount of money to the king and asked him to accept his sons as hostages and promised that he and his people would do as they were commanded, except only if he were compelled to come into his presence.[37] The king, more concerned with the interest of his people than with his stubbornness, received the hostages he was offered and granted that as a great favour the duke would not have to appear before

c. XI. Bretons and Beneventans subdued

him. Keeping the younger of the two sons as a hostage he sent the elder back to his father. He sent ambassadors with Arichis to demand and receive oaths of fidelity from the Beneventans. He went back to Rome and having spent several days worshipping at the holy places he returned to Gaul.

c. XII. Of the Bavarian war easily put to rest

11. Then the Bavarian war broke out suddenly and was brought to a swift end. It was caused by the pride and the weakness of Duke Tassilo.[38] His wife, who was the daughter of King Desiderius, urged him to it and thought she could take revenge for her father's exile through her husband. After he had made an alliance with the Huns, who live on the eastern frontier of the Bavarians, he tried not only to disobey the king's orders but to provoke him to war. The king's valour could not endure his defiance, which seemed excessive, and so he assembled troops from everywhere and invaded Bavaria and went with a great army to the River Lech. This river separates the Bavarians from the Alemannians. He pitched camp on the bank of the river, and decided to find out the duke's intentions by messengers before he entered the province. But Tassilo, thinking it would not be useful to himself or his people to act in a hostile fashion, humbly surrendered to the king, gave the hostages demanded, including his own son Theodo, and he also swore an oath that he would give way to anyone trying to persuade him to rebel.[39] And so this war, which seemed likely to be great, was brought to the swiftest end. But later Tassilo was summoned to the king and not allowed to return and the province which he ruled was no longer given to a duke but entrusted to counts.

c. XIII. How the Wilzi were subjugated

12. When these rebellions had been settled in this way war was declared against the Slavs, whom we are accustomed to call the Wiltzi[40] but who are correctly called the Welatabi in their own language. In that war the Saxons fought as auxiliaries among the other nations who followed the king's standards, though their obedience was feigned and lacking in loyalty. The cause of the war was that the Slavs were constantly attacking the Abrodites, who used to be allied with the Franks and could not be coerced by commands. A certain gulf of unknown length and a width which is

never more than a hundred miles and in many places much narrower, runs from the western ocean towards the east.[41] Many nations live around it: the Danes and Swedes, whom we call Northmen, live on the northern shore and all the islands in it. The Slavs and Estonians and various other nations live on the southern shore. The Welatabi are the chief among them, and war was made on them by the king. In a single expedition which he undertook he so defeated them and brought them under his rule that from that time they scarcely thought of refusing to do what he ordered.[42]

13. Apart from the war against the Saxons, the greatest of all the wars he waged was that which he undertook against the Avars or Huns, which followed this war. He managed it with greater vigour and a larger preparation than his other wars. He himself led one expedition into Pannonia, for that nation was dwelling in this province, the others he entrusted to his son Pippin, the governors of the provinces, the counts and even to representatives.[43] The war was administered by them most vigorously and completed in its eighth year. How many battles were fought, how much blood was shed, is attested by Pannonia, empty of all inhabitants, and the place where the palace of the Khan was, is so deserted that there is scarcely a trace of any human dwelling there. The whole nobility of the Avars perished in that war and all their glory ended. All the wealth and treasure they had assembled over many years was seized. Human memory cannot record any war against the Franks that left them richer and more enriched. Until that time they had seemed almost paupers but they found so much gold and silver in the palace and so much valuable booty was taken in the battles that the Franks might be thought to have justly taken from the Avars what the Avars had unjustly taken from other peoples. Only two of the leading Franks died in that war: Eric, the duke of Friuli, who was ambushed in Liburnia by the citizens of Tersatto, a city on the coast, and Gerold, the governor of Bavaria.[44] When he was about to engage in battle in Pannonia with the Avars he was killed, it is not known by whom, with two people who were riding with him and urging

c. XIV. The pride of the Huns, by what force it was mastered, and of the death of dukes Eric and Gerold

each man on. This war was almost without any other losses for the Franks and had a most successful ending, even though it lasted a long time because of its scale. After this, the Saxon war came to an end fitting to its duration. The Bohemian and Linonian wars came next, but could not last long. Both of them were brought to a swift end under the leadership of the younger Charles.

c. XV. The war against
the Northmen, how
it was begun and
put to rest

14. The last war was undertaken against the Northmen who are called Danes, firstly they engaged in piracy and then they raided the shores of Gaul and Germany with a larger fleet. Their king Godfrid was so filled with vain hope that he promised himself power over all of Germany. Indeed he thought of Frisia and Saxony as his own provinces. He had already brought his neighbours, the Abrodites, into his power and made them pay him tribute. He even boasted that he would soon come with a vast army to Aachen, where the king's court was. Although his boasts were most delusive they could not be completely refused credence, for it was thought that he was about to begin something like this, but he was stopped by sudden death. For he was slain by his own bodyguard, which ended both his life and the war he had begun.

c. XVI. How much
Charles added to
the kingdom of
the Franks by his
effort

15. These are the wars which the most powerful king waged with such prudence and success in various lands for forty-seven years, for he reigned that long. In those wars he so nobly increased the Frankish kingdom, which he had received from his father Pippin in a great and strong condition, that he nearly doubled its size. For previously no more land was occupied by the Franks who are called Eastern than that part of Gaul which lies between the Rhine, the Loire, the Atlantic ocean and the Balearic Sea, and that part of Germany bounded by Saxony and the rivers Danube, Rhine and Saale (which separates the Thuringians and the Sorbs). In addition to these, the Alemannians and the Bavarians belonged to the power of the Frankish kingdom. Charles himself, in the wars described, first added Aquitaine and Gascony and the whole range of the Pyrenees as far as the River Ebro, which has

its source in Navarre and flows through the most fertile plains of Spain and joins the Balearic Sea beneath the walls of the city of Tortosa; next he added all of Italy which stretches for more than a thousand miles from Aosta to lower Calabria,[45] which is the border between the Beneventans and the Greeks; then Saxony, which is no small part of Germany and is thought to be twice as wide as the land occupied by the Franks but similar to it in length; then he added both provinces of Pannonia and Dacia beyond the further bank of the Danube, and also Istria, Liburnia and Dalmatia save for its maritime cities, which he allowed the emperor of Constantinople to keep, because of the friendship and the pact between them. Then he subdued the uncivilized and wild nations who inhabit Germany between the Rhine and the Vistula rivers, the ocean and the Danube, to such an extent that he made them pay tribute. They almost all speak the same language but they are very different in customs and dress. The chief of these peoples are the Welatabi, Sorbs, Abrodites and Bohemians and he fought wars with them; the others, who far outnumber these, he received in surrender.

16. He also increased the glory of his kingdom by the friendship offered to him by certain kings and peoples. In this way he so won over Alfonso, the king of Galicia and Asturias, that when he sent letters or legates to Charles he ordered that in his presence the legates should only refer to him as Charles' subject.[46] By his generosity he had won over the Irish kings to his will so that they declared that he was nothing other than their lord and they were his servants and subjects. Letters which they sent to him survive and these attest to this sort of feeling towards him. He had such friendly relations to Harun-al-Rashid, the king of the Persians, who held almost all of the East except India, that he held him in favour more than all the kings and princes in the world and thought that he alone was worthy of his honour and generosity.[47] Indeed, when Charles's representatives, whom he had sent with gifts to the most holy sepulchre of our Lord and Saviour and to the place of His resurrection, came to him and told him of their lord's wishes, he not only allowed them

c. XVII. How he tried to win and to keep the friendship of foreign peoples

to do what they requested but even granted him that holy and salvific place so it might be thought to be in his power. He sent his own legates back and sent magnificent gifts to Charles, robes and spices and other riches of the East, and a few years before he had sent an elephant, the only one he possessed, to Charles, who had asked for one.[48] The emperors of Constantinople, Nicephorus, Michael and Leo,[49] who were seeking his friendship and alliance, sent him many ambassadors. But after he had taken up the name of emperor they suspected that he might want to seize their empire, so he established such a firm treaty with them that no source of any trouble might remain between them. For the power of the Franks was always suspect to the Romans and the Greeks; as the Greek proverb says: 'Have a Frank as a friend, not as a neighbour.'

c. XVIII. In which places he built wonderful works to ornament or defend his kingdom

17. This king, who showed himself so great in extending his empire and subduing foreign nations, and was constantly busy in that kind of activity, also undertook very many works calculated to adorn and benefit his kingdom, and brought several of them to completion. Among these, the most deserving of mention are the basilica of the Holy Mother of God at Aachen, built with wonderful skill, and a bridge over the Rhine at Mainz, five hundred paces long, for so wide is the river at this point.[50] This bridge was destroyed by fire the year before Charles died, but, because he died so soon after, it could not be repaired, although he had intended to rebuild it in stone in place of wood.[51] He began two palaces of beautiful workmanship – one not far from the city of Mainz in his villa called Ingelheim, the other at Nijmegen, on the River Waal, the stream that washes the south side of the island of the Batavians. But above all, sacred edifices were the object of his care throughout his whole kingdom; and whenever he found them falling into ruin from age, he commanded the priests and fathers who had charge of them to repair them, and made sure by commissioners that his instructions were obeyed.[52] He also fitted out a fleet for the war with the Northmen; the vessels required for this purpose were built on the rivers that flow from Gaul and Germany into the northern ocean. Moreover, since the

Northmen continually overran and laid waste the Gallic and German coasts, he caused watch and ward to be kept in all the harbours, and at the mouths of rivers large enough to admit the entrance of vessels, to prevent the enemy from disembarking. In the south, in Narbonensis and Septimania, and along the whole coast of Italy as far as Rome, he took the same precautions against the Moors, who had recently begun their piratical practices.[53] Hence, Italy suffered no great harm in his time at the hands of the Moors, nor Gaul and Germany from the Northmen, save that the Moors got possession of the Etrurian town of Civitavecchia by treachery, and sacked it,[54] and the Northmen harried some of the islands in Frisia, off the German coast.[55]

18. It is agreed that this was how he protected, increased and beautified his kingdom. From now on I should begin to speak of his gifts of mind and his supreme constancy in good and bad times and of those other things that belong to his private and domestic life.

After the death of his father, when he was sharing the kingdom with his brother, he endured the hostility and the jealousy of his brother with such great patience that it seemed wonderful to everyone that he could not provoke him to anger. Then at the urging of his mother he married a daughter of Desiderius, c. XIX. A summary of his domestic life and what wives and concubines and sons and daughters he had and how he taught them and about his mother and sister

the king of the Lombards, but for an uncertain reason he dismissed her after a year and married Hildegard, a very noble Swabian woman. By her he had three sons, Charles, Pippin and Louis, and as many daughters, Rotrud, Bertha and Gisela. He had three other daughters, Theodrada, Hiltrude and Rothaide, two of these by his own wife Fastrada, who was one of the Eastern Franks, that is, the Germans, and the third by a concubine, whose name now escapes me. On Fastrada's death he married Liutgard, an Alemannian woman, who had no children.[56] After her death he had three[57] concubines: Gersuinda, a Saxon, by whom he had a daughter named Adaltrude, and Regina, who gave birth to Drogo and Hugo and Adalinda who gave him Theoderic. Charles's mother Bertrada spent her old age in great honour with him. He treated her with the greatest reverence, so that there was never any quarrel between them, except over his divorce of the daughter of King Desiderius, whom he had married on her urging. She died after the death of Hildegard,[58] but had already seen three grandsons and the same number of granddaughters in her son's household. Charles had her buried with great honour in the same church in which his father lay, at St Denis. He had only one sister, named Gisela, who had devoted herself to the religious life from the time that she was a girl, and he treated her with great reverence, like his mother. She died a few years before his death in the monastery in which she had spent her life.[59]

19. He believed that his children should be brought up so that both sons and daughters were first educated in the liberal arts, which he himself had studied. Then when the sons had reached the right age he made them ride in the Frankish way, fight and hunt, and he ordered that his daughters learn to work wool with distaff and spindle, so that they might not grow dull in idleness and should spend their time in learning all virtuous activities.

c. XX. Which of his sons died before his own death and how he looked after the son and daughters of his son Pippin and what care he had for his sons and daughters

Of all his children he lost only two sons and one daughter before his own death: Charles, his eldest son,[60] Pippin, whom he had established as king of Italy,[61] and Rotrud, the eldest of his daughters, who had been engaged to Constantine, emperor of the Greeks.[62] Of these Pippin left one son, Bernard, and five daughters, Adelheid, Adela, Gundrada, Bertha and Theodrada. The king showed a special proof of his affection to them when after the death of his son he decreed that his grandson should succeed him and that the granddaughters be raised with his daughters. Despite his greatness of spirit he bore the death of his own sons and daughters with less patience, and his affection, which was no less, compelled him to weep. When he was informed of the death of Hadrian, the Roman pontiff, whom he held in great affection, he wept so much that it was as if he had lost a brother or a very dear son. He was by nature a good friend, for he made

friends easily and held on to them most constantly[63] and treated
those whom he had bound to himself in such friendship with
the greatest reverence.

He was so concerned for the education of his sons and daughters that he never dined without them when at home, and he
never journeyed without them. His sons rode with him, and his
daughters followed and at the end of their train some of his
followers were ordered to protect them. Although his daughters
were most beautiful and were deeply loved by him, strange to
say he never wanted to give any one of them in marriage to
anybody, whether a Frank or a foreigner, but kept them all
with him until his death, saying that he could not give up their
companionship. And because of this, though in other respects
happy he suffered the harshness of malign fortune. But he
concealed this so well that there was no suspicion of anything
shameful about them.

20. He also had a son named Pippin by a concubine whom I put off mentioning with the others;
he was fair of face but deformed by a hunchback.
When his father, who had taken up the war against

c. XXI. Of the two
conspiracies against
him, swiftly and
justly ended

the Avars, was wintering in Bavaria, he pretended to be ill and
plotted against his father with certain leading Franks, who had
won him over with the false promise of a kingdom.[64] When
their deceit was discovered and the conspirators condemned,
he was tonsured and allowed to embrace the religious life in
the monastery of Prüm. There had been a second powerful
conspiracy against him in Germany. All the perpetrators were
sent into exile, some blinded and others unharmed, but only
three conspirators lost their lives; since they had drawn their
swords to avoid arrest and had killed some people, they were
slain because there was no other way to subdue them. It is
thought that the cruelty of Queen Fastrada was the cause and
origin of these conspiracies. And so in both they conspired
against the king because he had consented to the cruelty of his
wife and seemed to have gone far beyond his usual kindness and gentleness. Otherwise, he passed his whole life with
the greatest love and esteem of everyone both at home and

abroad, so that no one ever complained of the least unjustified cruelty.

21. He loved foreigners and took great care in receiving them, so that their great number justifiably seemed a burden not only to the palace but also to the kingdom. But because of his greatness of soul he was scarcely affected by this, for the praise of his generosity and his good reputation repaid him for the great trouble.

c. XXII. Of the appearance of his body

22. His body was large and strong.[65] He was tall, but not unduly so, since his height was seven times the length of his own foot.[66] The top of his head was round, his eyes were large and lively, his nose was a little larger than average, he had fine white hair and a cheerful and attractive face.[67] So, standing or sitting his presence was greatly increased in authority and dignity. His neck seemed short and thick and his stomach seemed to project,[68] but the symmetry of the other parts hid these flaws.[69] His pace was firm and the whole bearing of his body powerful. Indeed his voice was clear but, given his size, not as strong as might have been expected. His health was good until four years before he died, when he suffered from constant fevers.[70] Towards the end he would limp on one foot.[71] Even then he trusted his own judgement more than the advice of his doctors, whom he almost hated, since they urged him to stop eating roast meat, which he liked, and to start eating boiled meats.[72]

c. XXIII. What activities he chiefly enjoyed

He exercised regularly by riding and hunting, which came naturally to him. Indeed there is hardly a people who can rival the Franks in this skill. He liked the steam of natural hot springs and the exercise that came from swimming. He was so good at swimming that no one was considered better than him. For this reason he built his palace at Aachen and lived there permanently during the last years of his life until he died. He invited to the baths not only his sons but also his nobles and friends, and sometimes he invited such a crowd of courtiers and bodyguards that there would be more than a hundred people bathing together.[73]

23. He used to wear his national, that is, Frankish, costume; close to his body he put on a linen shirt and linen underwear, then a tunic c. XXIV. What clothes he was accustomed to wear fringed with silk and stockings, then he wrapped his thighs and his feet with stockings, and covered his shoulders and chest in winter with a jacket made of otter-skin or ermine and a blue cloak, and he was always armed with his sword, which had a gold or silver hilt and belt. Sometimes he used a jewelled sword, but only at great feast days or when he received foreign ambassadors. He spurned foreign clothes, even the most beautiful, and never wore them except at Rome, when, asked once by Pope Hadrian and then by his successor Leo, he wore a long tunic and a chlamys and put on shoes made in the Roman way. On feast days he would process wearing a robe woven of gold and jewelled leggings and fastened his cloak with a golden brooch, and wore a crown of gold adorned with jewels. But on other days his costume was little different from that of the common people.[74]

24. Moderate in his food and drink, he was more moderate when it came to drink, since he very much hated to see anyone drunk, and especially himself and his own household. But c. XXV. What kind of food, drink and sleep he had and what he used to do between meals he was not able to abstain from food, and often complained that fasting was bad for his health.[75] He used to feast very rarely, and only on special holidays, but then with a large number of people. At his meal each day only four courses were prepared, in addition to the roast, which the hunters[76] were accustomed to serve on spits and which was his favourite dish. While eating he listened either to a performer[77] or to someone reading out the histories and deeds of the ancients. He enjoyed the books of St Augustine, especially those entitled the *City of God*.[78] He was so restrained in his drinking of wine and any sort of drink that he rarely drank more than three times at a meal. In summer, after the midday meal he would take some fruit and take a single drink, then he would take off his clothes and shoes as if it were night and would rest for two or three hours. At night he slept so that he not only woke but also got

up four or five times.[79] While putting on his shoes and dressing
he not only saw friends but if the count of the palace said that
there was some dispute which could not be resolved without
his judgement he would order him to bring the disputants and,
as if sitting in court, he heard the dispute and gave judgement.
He not only did this at that time but whatever on that day
needed to be handled or whatever was to be requested of any
of his officials was dealt with.

c. XXVI. Of the   25. He was rich in eloquence and was able to
wonderful vigilance   express most clearly whatever he wished to say.
of his studies
                              He was not simply content with his native tongue
but even spent time learning foreign languages. Of these he
learned Latin well enough to pray in it as much as in his own
native language, but he was able to understand Greek better
than he could speak it. He was so fluent that he even seemed
verbose.[80] He cultivated the liberal arts most studiously and,
greatly respecting those who taught them, he granted them
great honours. In learning grammar he followed Peter of Pisa,
an elderly deacon. For the other disciplines he had as his teacher
Alcuin, called Albinus, a deacon from Britain of the race of the
Saxons, a man who in any place would have been thought most
learned.[81] With him he spent much time and effort learning
rhetoric and dialectic, and especially astronomy.

He learned the art of calculation and with concentrated learning and precision he investigated the movement of the stars. He
tried to learn to write and for this reason he put tablets and
notebooks under the pillows in his bed so that if he had any
free time he could accustom his hand to forming letters; but his
effort, begun too late, achieved little.

c. XXVII. How   26. With great piety and devotion he practised
much he increased   the Christian religion in which he had been reared
the splendour of
the Church   from infancy. For this reason he constructed a
                              church of great beauty at Aachen and adorned it
with gold and silver and lamps, and with railings and portals
made of solid bronze.[82] Since he could not procure columns
and marble from anywhere else he took the trouble to have
them brought from Rome and Ravenna. As long as his health
allowed, he regularly went to church both morning and evening,

and also to the night offices and to Mass. He was especially
concerned that everything done in the church should be done
with the greatest dignity and he frequently warned the sacristans
that nothing foul or unclean should be brought into the church
or left there. He supplied the church with such an abundance
of sacred vessels made of gold and silver and with such a great
number of clerical vestments that in the celebration of the
Mass not even the janitors, who hold the lowest of all the
ecclesiastical orders, found it necessary to serve in their ordinary
clothes. He corrected the discipline of reading and singing most
carefully, for he was skilled in both. But he himself never read
publicly and would only sing in a low voice with the rest of the
congregation.

27. He was very enthusiastic in supporting
the poor, and in that spontaneous generosity
which the Greeks call alms, so much so that he
made a point of not only giving in his own country and his own
kingdom, but even overseas when he discovered that there were
Christians living in poverty in Syria, Egypt and Africa; and at
Jerusalem, Alexandria and Carthage he had compassion on
their wants, and used to send money.[83] The reason that he
zealously strove to make friends with the kings beyond seas
was that he might get some help and relief to the poor Christians
living under their rule.

c. XXVIII. How generous he was in almsgiving

He cherished the church of St Peter the
Apostle at Rome above all other holy and
sacred places. He gave its treasury a vast wealth
of gold, silver and precious stones. He sent
great and countless gifts to the popes; and
throughout his whole reign he considered nothing more important than to re-establish the ancient authority of the city of
Rome by his care and by his influence, and not only to defend
and protect the church of St Peter, but to beautify and enrich it
out of his own store above all other churches. Although he held
it in such veneration, he only went to Rome to pay his vows
and to pray four times during the whole forty-seven years that
he reigned.[84]

c. XXIX. With what love he cared for the Roman see and how he was elevated by the imperial title

28. The reasons for his last visit were not just these, but rather because the residents of Rome had inflicted many injuries on Pope Leo, putting out his eyes and cutting off his tongue. This forced him to appeal to the loyalty of the king. Thus Charles travelled to Rome to restore the state of the Church, which was extremely disturbed, and he spent the whole winter there. It was at this time that he received the title of Emperor and Augustus. At first he disliked this so much that he said that he would not have entered the church that day, even though it was a great feast day, if he had known in advance of the pope's plan. But he bore the animosity that the assumption of this title caused with great patience, for the Roman emperors were angry about it. He overcame their opposition through his greatness of spirit, which was without doubt far greater than theirs, by often sending ambassadors to them and by calling them his brothers in his letters.

c. XXX. Of his care in emending the laws

29. After he had taken the imperial title, since he saw that many things were lacking in the laws of his people (for the Franks have two laws,[85] very different in many places), he thought of supplying what was lacking and reconciling their differences and of correcting what was bad or wrongly expressed. But he did nothing more than add a few chapters to the law, and they were unfinished. He did, however, order that the laws of all the peoples under his rule which were not written should be written down.[86] He also ordered that the very old German songs, in which the deeds and wars of ancient kings were celebrated, should be written down and preserved. He also began a grammar of his native language.

c. XXXI. With what new names he designated the months, the years and the twelve winds

He gave names to the months in his native language, since before that time the Franks had given partly German and partly Latin names. He also gave individual names to the twelve winds, since until then scarcely more than four of them had been named. And he called January *Wintarmanoth*, February *Hornung*, March *Lentzinmanoth*, April *Ostarmanoth*, May *Winnemanoth*, June *Brachmanoth*, July *Heuuimanoth*, August *Aranmanoth*, September *Witumanoth*, October *Windumemanoth*, November *Herbistmanoth*, December *Heilagmanoth*.[87] He gave the winds these names: the east wind *Ostroniwint*, the east-south wind *Ostsundroni*, the south-east wind *Sundostroni*, the south wind *Sundroni*, the south-west wind *Sundwestroni*, the west-south wind *Westsundroni*, the west wind *Westroni*, the west-north wind *Westnordroni*, the north-west wind *Nordwestroni*, the north wind *Nordroni*, the north-east wind *Nordostroni* and the east-north wind *Ostnordroni*.[88]

30. At the very end of his life when he was worn down by ill-health and old age, he summoned his son Louis, king of Aquitaine, the only one of his sons by Hildegard to survive, *c. XXXII. How he made his son Louis heir to the imperial power and name* and gathered together all the chief men of the whole kingdom of the Franks in a solemn assembly. He appointed Louis, with their unanimous consent, to rule with himself over the whole kingdom and made him heir to the imperial name; placing the diadem upon his son's head, he ordered that he should be called Emperor and Augustus. This decision was hailed by all present with great approval, for it seemed as if God had prompted him to it for the kingdom's good; it increased his majesty, and struck no little terror into foreign nations. After sending his son back to Aquitaine, although weak from age he set out to hunt, as usual, not far from his palace at Aachen, and passed the rest of the autumn in this way, returning to Aachen about 1 November.

While wintering there, he was seized in the month of January with a high fever and took to his bed. As soon as he was taken sick, he *c. XXXIII. The death and burial of the great emperor Charles* prescribed for himself abstinence from food, as he always used to do in case of fever, thinking that the disease could be driven off, or at least mitigated, by fasting. Besides the fever, he suffered from a pain in the side, which the Greeks call pleurisy; but he still persisted in fasting, and in keeping up his strength only by very infrequent drinks. He died on 28 January, the seventh day from the time that he took to his bed, at nine o'clock in the morning, after partaking of the Holy Communion, in the seventy-second year of his age and the forty-seventh of his reign.

31. His body was solemnly washed and prepared and, to the great grief of all the people, brought into the church and buried there. At first there was uncertainty as to where it should be placed, because while alive he had specified nothing. Finally everyone agreed that he could be buried nowhere more suitably than in that basilica which he had built at his own expense for the love of God and our Lord Jesus Christ and to honour His mother, the holy and eternal Virgin. He was buried there on the same day on which he died and a golden arch was erected over his tomb with an image and an inscription. The inscription was written as follows: 'UNDER THIS TOMB LIES THE BODY OF CHARLES, THE GREAT AND ORTHODOX EMPEROR, WHO GLORIOUSLY INCREASED THE KINGDOM OF THE FRANKS AND REIGNED WITH GREAT SUCCESS FOR FORTY-SEVEN YEARS. HE DIED IN HIS SEVENTIES IN THE YEAR OF OUR LORD 814, IN THE SEVENTH INDICTION, ON THE TWENTY-EIGHTH DAY OF JANUARY.'

c. XXXIV. Of the portents which foretold his death

32. There were so many portents of his approaching death that not only others but even he himself felt it was threatening. For three successive years near the end of his life there were frequent eclipses of the sun and moon and a dark spot was seen on the sun for seven days.[89] The portico which he had constructed between the church and palace suddenly fell to the ground on Ascension Day.[90] The bridge across the Rhine at Mainz, which he had been building for ten years with great effort and remarkable skill and out of wood in such a way that it seemed it might last for ever, accidentally caught fire and burned down in three hours so that not a single splinter remained, except what was covered by the water.

When Charlemagne was on his last expedition in Saxony against Godfrid, the king of the Danes, one day when he had left the camp before sunrise he saw a shooting star with a great light fall from the sky from right to left through clear air, and while everyone was wondering what this sign might mean the horse he was riding suddenly lowered its head and fell, throwing him to the ground so hard that the brooch of his cloak broke and his sword-belt came off. His servants hurried up and raised him, disarmed and without his cloak. The spear that he had been holding tightly in his hand fell so that it lay twenty feet or more distant. Added to these were the frequent tremors in the palace at Aachen and the constant creaking in the ceiling panels of the buildings in which he lived. The church in which he was later buried was struck by lightning, and the golden apple which stood at the peak of the roof was struck by lightning and landed on the cornice of the bishop's house, which was next to the church. In that church was an inscription in red letters, between the upper and lower arches along the inside of the building, that gave the name of the builder of that church.[91] In the last line of that inscription *Karolus Princeps* could be read, but it was observed by some people that in the very year he died, a few months before his death, the letters that formed *Princeps* became so faint that they were almost invisible. Yet Charles either rejected all these things or acted as if none of them were related to his affairs in any way.

33. He decided to make a will by which he would make his daughters and the offspring of his concubines his heirs, but he began this late and could not finish it. However, three years before he died he made the division of his treasures, his fortune, his clothes and his other furnishings, in the presence of his friends and servants, instructing them that after his death the distribution made by him should be carried out, and he set out in a note what he wished to be done with the things he had divided up. The text and sense of this note went as follows:

c. XXXV. Of the division of his treasures

In the name of the omnipotent Lord God, the Father, Son and Holy Spirit, this inventory and division was made by the most glorious and most pious Lord Charles, Emperor Augustus, in the 811th year of the Incarnation of our Lord Jesus Christ, in the 43rd year of his reign in Francia and 36th in Italy, the 11th of his empire, and the 4th Indiction, which pious and prudent thought have determined him, and the favour of God enabled him, to make of his treasures and money found in his chamber on this day. In this division he was especially desirous to provide not only that the gift of alms which Christians usually make of their own possessions shall be made for himself in due course and order out of his wealth, but also that his heirs shall be free from all doubt, and know clearly what should belong to them, and be able to share their property by suitable partition without litigation or dispute.

c. XXXVI. The first two parts were given to holy places

With this intention and to this end he has first divided all his substance and movable goods found to be in his chamber on the day mentioned, in gold, silver, precious stones and royal ornaments into three lots. Then he subdivided two of the lots into twenty-one parts, keeping the third whole. The first two lots have been thus subdivided into twenty-one parts because there are twenty-one metropolitan cities in his kingdom, and in order that each archbishopric may receive one of the said parts by way of alms, at the hands of Charlemagne's heirs and friends, and that the archbishop who shall then administer its affairs shall take the part given to his church, and share the same with his suffragans, in such manner that one-third shall go to the Church and the remaining two-thirds be divided among the suffragans. The twenty-one parts into which the first two lots are to be distributed, according to the number of recognized metropolitan cities, have been set apart one from another and each has been put aside by itself in a box labelled with the name of the city for which it is destined. The names of the cities to which these alms or gifts are to be sent are as follows: Rome, Ravenna, Milan, Friuli, Grado, Cologne, Mainz, Salzburg, Trier, Sens, Besançon, Lyons, Rouen, Reims, Arles, Vienne, Moûtiers-en-Tarantaise, Embrun, Bordeaux, Tours and Bourges.

c. XXXVII. To what the third part was directed

The third portion, which he wishes to be kept whole, is to be bestowed as follows: While the first two lots are to be divided into the parts aforesaid, and set aside under seal, the third lot shall be employed for the owner's daily needs, as property which he shall be under no obligation to part with for the fulfilment of any vow, and this as long as he shall be alive, or consider it necessary for his use. But upon his death, or voluntary renunciation of the affairs of this world, this lot shall be divided into four parts, and one of them shall be added to the twenty-one parts; the second shall be assigned to his sons and daughters, and to the sons and daughters of his sons, to be distributed among them in just and equal partition; the third, in accordance with the custom common among Christians, shall be devoted to the poor; and the fourth shall go to the support of the menservants and maidservants on duty at the palace. It is his wish that to this said third lot of the whole amount, which also consists of gold and silver, shall be added all the vessels and utensils of bronze, iron and other metals, together with the arms, clothing and other movable goods, costly and cheap, used for various purposes such as hangings, rugs, woollen stuffs, felts, leather articles and saddles in order that thus the parts of the said lot may be augmented, and the alms distributed reach more people.

He ordains that his chapel – that is to say, its church property, both that which he has provided and collected as well as that which came to him by inheritance from his father – shall remain entire, and not be separated by any division whatever. If, however, any vessels, books or other adornments be found therein which are certainly known not to have been given by him to that chapel, whoever wants them shall have them on paying their value at a fair estimation. He likewise commands that the books which he has collected in his library in great numbers shall be sold for a fair price to those who want them, and the money received given to the poor.

c. XXXVIII. What he decreed about his chapel and his books

It is well known that among the other treasures and money there are three silver tables, and one very large and massive golden one. He directs and commands that the square table, upon which there is a representation of the city of Constantinople, shall be sent to the basilica of St Peter the Apostle at Rome, with the other gifts destined for it; that the round one, adorned with a likeness of the city of Rome, shall be given to the episcopal church at Ravenna; and that the third, which far surpasses the other two in weight and in beauty of workmanship, and showing the plan of the whole universe in three circles, drawn with skill and delicacy, shall go, together with the golden table, fourthly above men-

c. XXXIX. About the three silver and the fourth gold table

tioned, to increase that lot which is to be devoted to his heirs and to alms.[92]

This deed, and the dispositions thereof, he has made and appointed in the presence of the bishops, abbots and counts able to be present, whose names are hereto subscribed. Bishops: Hildebald, Richolf, Arno, Wolfar, Bernoin, Laidrad, John, Theodulf, Jesse, Heito, Waltgaud.[93] Abbots: Fredugis, Adalung, Angilbert, Irmino.[94] Counts: Wala, Meginher, Otulf, Stephen, Unruoch, Burchard, Meginhard,[95] Hatto, Rihwin, Edo, Ercangar, Gerold, Bero, Hildigern, Rocculf.

His son Louis, who succeeded him by divine command, having examined this document took care that all these things were done as quickly as possible after his death with the greatest zeal.

NOTKER
THE STAMMERER

THE DEEDS OF
CHARLEMAGNE

Introduction

The poet Notker the Stammerer was born around 840 in Jonswil in the canton of St Gall in modern Switzerland, where his brother Othere was a chief official. He entered the monastery of St Gall as a boy and remained there as a monk until his death on 6 April 912.[1] Chief among his pupils at the monastic school were Salomon, later abbot of St Gall and bishop of Konstanz 891–920, and Salomon's brother Waldo, bishop of Freising in Bavaria. Notker composed a Life of St Gall in the form of a dialogue in prose and verse divided into three books, dedicated to Hartmann, monk and later abbot of St Gall, of which only fragments have survived. In 884 he dedicated a collection of some fifty verse compositions with melodies, organized in a cycle for the Church year, to Bishop Liutward of Vercelli, the chancellor of the emperor Charles the Fat. He also composed poems of friendship. These works have been described as 'the product of one of the few great poets between the Gospels and Dante',[2] and Notker was a major composer of early medieval liturgical music. In 896 he revised the *Martyrology*, listing the saints to be commemorated on each day of the year and composed by Bishop Ado of Vienne in 858,[3] and wrote a letter to Salomon discussing the works which should be studied by the young.[4] In addition, he copied charters for the abbey from 870 to 892, and his autograph notes are found in the ninth-century library catalogue.[5]

His wit is recorded in his own works, but also in the history of the abbey of St Gall composed by Ekkehard IV around 1030. Ekkehard remembered Notker in the following words:

Notker was frail in body, though not in mind, a stammerer in
voice but not in spirit; lofty in divine thoughts, patient in adversity, gentle in everything, strict in enforcing the discipline of our
convent, yet somewhat timid in sudden and unexpected alarms,
except in the assaults of demons, whom he always withstood
manfully. He was most assiduous in illuminating, reading, and
composing; and (that I may embrace all his gifts of holiness
within a brief compass) he was a vessel of the Holy Ghost, as full
as any other of his own time.[6]

The *Gesta Karoli* (Deeds of Charlemagne) was begun as a
work in three books after Charles the Fat's visit to St Gall on
4–8 December 883, and on several occasions Notker addresses
Charles directly in his work. Since Charles was deposed in
November 887 the *Gesta* must have been composed between
883 and 887. Simon MacLean has recently argued that we can
date it more precisely, between 885 and early 887.[7] Only two
books survive, and the manuscripts break off in the middle of
a story about Charlemagne's son Louis the Pious and his jester.
The work is anonymous, but the author calls himself *balbus et
edentulus* (toothless and stammering) in chapter 17 of Book II
and Notker calls himself 'unworthy Notker the Stammerer' in
his sequence on St Stephen and 'stammering and toothless' in a
letter to Waldo and Salomon.

In the *Gesta*, Notker tells us how, as a boy, he was brought
up by the old warrior Adalbert, who used to tell him stories
about Charlemagne and his wars. Charlemagne is presented as a
mythical figure, judging and rewarding schoolboys, appointing
bishops, feasting, hunting and fighting. His virtues are simplicity and courage, he mocks those courtiers who wear fine
fancy garments. And he leads an army able to conquer the
world, as the story of the siege of Pavia makes clear. Unlike
Einhard's hero, Notker's Charlemagne looks down from his
palace balcony like God himself and knows the threats to his
empire. There are splendid tales about the baptism of Vikings,
the order of court ceremonial and gift-giving. But there are also
the perennial themes of religious life: sin and penance, the work
of the devil and miracles, and the relations between the emperor

and his bishops. Notker knew that empires were transient. He was aware of the threat posed by overmighty subjects of his own time, those whom he called a 'devilish group of conspirators' (II.12), who scorn the Carolingian line.

His book is redolent of the schoolroom, with learned references to pagan gods and donkeys compared to dolphins. The Bible is ever present, from the opening image of Nebuchadnezzar's statue to the apostolic injunction which Louis the Pious follows in supplying all needs by his almsgiving in the final story. Human history is presented and understood as a part of divine history. But Notker conveys history by means of the anecdote, telling stories designed to stick in the memory and to delight their audience. He was probably writing for readers who had read Einhard's biography, which was studied in several Carolingian monasteries, and chose to subvert the secular features of Einhard's book by imposing his own categories so that piety precedes wars, and by starting with two Irishmen selling wisdom instead of an oxcart.[8]

The earliest surviving manuscripts of the *Gesta* date from the twelfth century, and all lack the preface to Book I (mentioned in the preface to Book II) and break off in or before chapter 21 of Book II, though in chapter 16 of Book II Notker says he intended to write a book on Charlemagne's piety and care of the church, his wars, and the daily life of Charlemagne. 'If I do not curtail somewhat his feats in war, I shall never come to consider his daily habits of life.' The text is incomplete, possibly because Notker abandoned the work on Charles's death, and the text as we have it may omit some of Notker's intentions.

All but two of the manuscripts combine Notker's text with Einhard's Life, and Notker follows Einhard in offering a thematic rather than a historical narrative. But, rather than with the Merovingians, he starts with God who ordains the fate of kingdoms, with wisdom rather than power, and with Charlemagne's concern for the church rather than with his wars. We know that Einhard's biography was read in monastic schools: Notker is providing his own commentary on the work by transforming its priorities. His ruler is concerned with correct

worship, with educating future abbots and bishops. Proud clerics are humbled. The emperor is God's earthly representative,
and has divine features. He is called the friend of God and the
most just judge after God. He is compared to David and, in his
building programme at Aachen, to Solomon. The Franks were
often treated as the successors to the Israelites, the 'new people
of God'[9] and their rulers were compared to David and Solomon
by Alcuin and Angilbert.[10]

The *Gesta* was composed for Charles the Fat and offered him
and his family examples of how to rule. 'Your own father
imitated this example ... throughout his life,' he says (II. 17).
There are repeated references to Charles's command to write
it: 'through my desire to obey your orders I may incur the
enmity of all who have taken vows' (I. 18), for example. Charles
is urged to fight the Vikings (II. 14) and chapters 16 and 17 of
Book II make mention of 'your most glorious father Louis' and
'your most religious father imitated this example' by wearing
iron, and of the gifts of Louis the German. The work focuses
on Charlemagne as a heroic and most wise ruler, describing
him in a string of superlatives. But Notker calls his work a
history, and sets Charlemagne's achievement within a divine
plan in which the Franks succeed the Romans. In Notker's
idealized world, merit is rewarded, and the emperor has become
a larger-than-life hero, the most just judge after God, and the
bishop of bishops. Notker tells us that he relied on the tales
which he heard from the priest Werinbert and his father Adalbert, who had fought in Charlemagne's wars against Avars,
Saxons and Slavs. He tells a story about the Avar campaign
which he learned from the giant warrior Eishere from the
Thurgau. But his work is a skilled literary composition. He
frequently uses biblical quotations, and has borrowed several
phrases from Virgil. He quotes from the Life of Antony by
Athanasius (356–62), the Life of St Ambrose by Paulinus
(397) and the Life of St Martin by Sulpicius Severus (before
397), and he knew the Lives of the St Gall saints Gallus and
Otmar. In addition, his vocabulary draws on the Christian poet
and school author Prudentius (348–413), on letters of Alcuin
and on the works for monks composed by John Cassian (360–

433). He quotes Augustine on the Trinity when telling about the baptism of Vikings. He has an inaccurate reference to Bede's *Ecclesiastical History*. His account of how the kings of the Franks venerated the cloak of St Martin comes from Walahfrid Strabo. Copies of all of these texts were in the St Gall library (some can be seen on the website Codices Electronici Sangallenses). But his main source was Einhard's Life of Charlemagne, and his work can be seen as an attempt to provide a revision of Einhard's text, with a proper emphasis, lacking in Einhard, on Charlemagne as Christian ruler and a part of the divine plan for salvation.

Professor Lewis Thorpe, who first produced a Penguin Classics translation of these two works in 1969, contrasted Einhard and Notker in these words:

> Einhard knew Charlemagne intimately: he had been at his court for some twenty-three years. The Monk of Saint Gall, who had seen Charles the Fat for some three days only, was writing seventy years after the death of Charlemagne. Despite this, the Charlemagne of Einhard remains a stiff figure, a deified Roman Emperor, while the Charlemagne of the Monk of Saint Gall seems to live before our eyes and to be a little nearer to the real man whom we find portrayed elsewhere. He rounds in fury on the young noblemen who pay lip-service to learning and give little attention to the teaching of Clement. When he is chiding his courtiers for their useless finery, he calls for his own rough jacket: 'Give that sheepskin of mine a rub between your fingers,' says he to his servant, as might Montgomery in the Western Desert, 'and then bring it in for me to look at.'

Thorpe was a Professor of French who had served with distinction in the Second World War, and who was much closer to Charlemagne's world than I am. He was interested in Charlemagne as a hero of much Old French literature, beginning with the *Song of Roland*, and saw Notker as the first to record stories about Charlemagne. He painted a charming picture of Notker 'warming [his] bones on the rustic seats in the monastery garden' and telling good old familiar stories. Later scholars have suggested that the stories were told to criticize Notker's contemporaries, but they have not challenged Thorpe's sense that these stories are more vivid and memorable than Einhard's classicizing booklet. Notker's work, though unfinished, is twice as long as Einhard's.

Notker is more vivid because he can break free of Einhard's scheme. But he can only do that because he is writing for readers who have read Einhard, readers who need to be taught moral lessons about the world outside the monastery walls. The lessons often reinforce Notker's values, rather than those of Charlemagne, but they offer a reading of Einhard and Charlemagne far closer to both men by date of composition, but also by mindset, than our own views can be. It is a measure of Einhard's remarkable achievement that his Life offered a challenge to the monks of St Gall: it seemed too secular in its values, and it seemed to leave God out of history. But Einhard's account of the portents before Charlemagne's death make it clear that he thought that God does rule history, though we cannot understand how.

The text was first edited by Hermann Canisius in 1601, and Canisius correctly ascribed it to Notker. Here it is translated from the revised edition made by Hans Haefele for the *Monumenta Germaniae Historica, Scriptores Rerum Germanicarum*, Nova Series, 12 (Munich, 1980).

NOTES

1. The best introduction to the culture of the abbey in English can be found in the various essays in J. C. King (ed.), *Sangallensia in Washington: The Arts and Letters in Medieval and Baroque St Gall Viewed from the Late Twentieth Century* (New York, 1994). See also Codices Electronici Sangallenses, http://www. cesg.unifr.ch/en/, which will include digitized images of all the manuscripts from St Gall.

2. W. von den Steinen, *Notker der Dichter und seine geistige Welt*, 2 vols. (Berne, 1948), vol. 1, p. 7. The second volume of this work is an edition and translation of Notker's *Liber Ymnorum*.

3. John M. McCulloh, 'Historical Martyrologies in the Benedictine

Cultural Tradition', *Mediaevalia Lovaniensia*, series 1 (Studia), 11 (1983), pp. 114–31.

4. E. Rauner, 'Notkers des Stammlers "Notatio de illustribus viris" ' *Mittellatches Jahrbuch*, 21 (1986), pp. 34–69.

5. For illustrations, see S. Rankin, 'Ego itaque Notker scripsi', *Revue bénédictine*, 101 (1991), pp. 268–98.

6. Ekkehard von St Gallen, *Casus Sancti Galli*, chapter 38, trans. in G. C. Coulton (ed.), *A Medieval Garner* (London, 1910), pp. 18–19.

7. See Simon Maclean, *Kingship and Politics in the Late Ninth Century: Charles the Fat and the End of the Carolingian Empire* (Cambridge, 2003), pp. 201–4.

8. David Ganz, 'Humour as History in Notker's *Gesta Karoli Magni*', in E. King, J. Schaefer and W. Wadley (eds.), *Monks, Nuns and Friars in Medieval Society* (Sewanee, Tem., 1989), pp. 171–83.

9. 1 Peter 2: 10.

10. See Mary Garrison, 'The Franks as the New Israel? Education for an Identity from Pippin to Charlemagne', in Y. Hen and M. Innes, *The Uses of the Past in the Early Middle Ages* (Cambridge, 2000), pp. 114–63.

THE FIRST BOOK OF THE
DEEDS OF CHARLES

1. The omnipotent disposer of all things and the director of kingdoms and of the ages, when he had destroyed that wondrous statue with feet of iron or of clay among the Romans,[1] set up the golden head of another no less remarkable statue among the Franks through the illustrious Charlemagne. When he had begun to rule alone in the western parts of the world, and the study of letters was everywhere almost forgotten, so that the worship of the true God was weak, it happened that two Scots from Ireland[2] came with British traders to the shore of Gaul, and they were men most wonderfully instructed both in secular and in sacred texts. When they displayed nothing for sale, they used to shout to the crowds who had come to buy things: 'If anyone is eager for wisdom, let him come to us and receive it, for that is what we have for sale.' They claimed that they had it for sale because they saw that the people were trading in what was priced rather than what was free, so they could either spur them to buy wisdom just like the other things they were buying; or else, as subsequent events proved, by such an announcement they provoked wonder and amazement. They proclaimed these things for such a long time that finally the onlookers, thinking them crazy, brought the matter to the ears of King Charles, who was always a most greedy lover of wisdom. He summoned them to his presence with the utmost speed and asked them if it was true, as rumour had it, that they had brought wisdom with them. They said: 'Yes indeed we have it, and in the name of the Lord we are ready to give it to those who seek it in a proper way.' When he had asked them what they wanted for it, they replied: 'We only ask for a suitable

place and talented minds and food and clothing, without which
our pilgrimage cannot be accomplished.' When he received this
answer he was filled with great joy and first he kept them both
with him for a short time. Later, when he was compelled to
go on military campaigns he ordered one of them, named
Clement,[3] to live in Gaul, and he entrusted to him many boys
very noble and middling and wretched, and ordered that they
be fed and given suitable places to live. The second, who was
called < . . . >,[4] he sent to Italy and granted him the monastery
of St Augustine near the city of Pavia, so that whoever wished
might gather there to be taught by him.

2. When Alcuin,[5] of the nation of the English, heard how
eagerly Charles, the most devout of rulers, received wise men,
he boarded a ship and came to him. He was more skilled in all
the breadth of writings than other men of modern times, being
a pupil of the most learned Bede, the most learned interpreter
of the Scriptures since St Gregory. He kept him constantly at
his side until the end of his life, except when he went to mighty
wars, to such an extent that he wanted to be called his pupil
and to call Alcuin his teacher. He gave him the abbey of
St Martin near the city of Tours, so that when he was away
Alcuin could rest there and teach those who flocked to him.[6]
His teaching was so fruitful that the modern Gauls or Franks
equalled the ancient Romans or Athenians.[7]

3. When the most victorious Charles after a long time
returned to Gaul he ordered the boys he had entrusted to
Clement to come to him and to offer him their letters and
poems. Those of middling and low rank offered them sweetened
with all the savours of wisdom, more than anyone could have
hoped for. But the nobles offered work full of all fatuity. Then
the most wise Charles, imitating the justice of the eternal judge,
placed those who had worked well on his right and said to
them: 'Many thanks, my sons, for you have worked hard to
carry out my order and to do what is useful to you as best
you could. Now strive to reach perfection and I will give you
splendid bishoprics and monasteries and you will always be
honoured in my sight.' Then he turned to those on his left with
great hostility, twisting his face, and pierced their consciences

with his fiery gaze, and ironically he thundered rather than spoke these dread words to them: 'You nobles, you sons of my leading men, soft and dandified, trusting in your birth and your wealth, paying no attention to my command and to your advancement, you neglected the pursuit of learning and indulged yourselves in the sport of pleasure and idleness and foolish pastimes.' When he had said this, turning his august head and his unconquered right hand to heaven he thundered forth an oath. 'By the King of the heavens I think nothing of your nobility and your beauty. Others can admire you. Know this without any doubt; unless you rapidly make up for your idleness by eager effort,[8] you will never receive any benefit from Charlemagne.'

4. From the poor I have mentioned above he chose one who was an excellent secretary and writer for his chapel.[9] This is what the kings of the Franks are accustomed to call their holy place, from the *cappa* of St Martin, which they always carry with them to war for their protection and to crush their enemies.[10] When it was announced to the most far-sighted king Charles that a certain bishop had died and he asked if he had left anything from his possessions or his efforts, the messenger answered: 'Lord he has left no more than two pounds of silver.' The young man sighed and was unable to keep his thought to himself but with the king listening he burst out unwillingly: 'A small provision for a long and eternal journey.' When the most controlled of men Charles had thought for a little he said to him: 'Do you think that if you were to accept that bishopric, you would take care to make more provision for that long journey?'[11] He immediately devoured those words as if they were the first ripe grapes falling into his gaping mouth, fell at his feet and said: 'Lord, this lies in God's will and in your power.' And the king said: 'Stand behind the curtain which hangs at my back and hear how many helpers you will have for this honour.' When the courtiers, always on the watch for the falls or even the deaths of others, heard of the death of the bishop, they tried hard to get the bishopric for themselves through the people close to the emperor, each of them impatient of delays and everyone envying everyone else. But he, remaining

immutable in his counsel,[12] refused it to everyone, saying that
he did not want to lie to that young man. At last Queen Hildegard first sent the nobles of the kingdom to the king and then
came in person to ask for that bishopric for her cleric. And
when he had listened most cheerfully to her request he said that
he would not and could not refuse her anything, but he did not
want to disappoint his little cleric. It is the custom of all women
to want their own plan and wish to prevail over the decisions
of their husbands, so, concealing the anger in her mind and
turning her loud voice into a feeble one, with faint movements
she tried to weaken the unchanged resolve of the emperor. She
said to him: 'My lord king, why should the boy have the bishopric to waste it? But I beg you, my sweetest lord, my glory and
my refuge,[13] that you give it to your faithful servant my own
cleric.' Then the young man whom the king had ordered to
stand behind the curtain near to where he himself was sitting
(so he could hear how each of them begged for it) embracing
Charlemagne, curtain and all, burst into this lament: 'Lord
king, keep your resolution, lest anyone snatch from your hands
the power vested in you by God.' Then that strongest lover of
truth called him out into the open and said to him: 'You shall
have that bishopric and take care that you prepare great
expenses and a provision for that long and irrevocable journey
which lies before you and me.'

5. There was a certain cleric in the royal retinue, who was
poor and low spirited and not adequately trained in the study
of letters. The most pious Charles, taking pity on his poverty,
even though everyone hated him and wanted to drive him away,
could never be persuaded to drive him away or remove him
from his retinue. It happened on the vigil of the feast of
St Martin that the death of a certain bishop was announced to
the emperor. He summoned one of his clerics, not a little
endowed with nobility and learning, and gave him that bishopric. The cleric was so overjoyed that he invited many courtiers
to his quarters and received many people who had come from
his diocese with great splendour and had a splendid feast prepared for everyone. 'Heavy with the banquet, drowned in drink
and buried by wine',[14] on that most holy night he failed to come

to the night office. It was the custom that on the day before the master of the choir arranged with everyone which responsory they were to sing. But he, who now virtually held a bishopric in his grasp, was charged with the responsory *Domine si adhuc populo tuo sum necessarius*. Since he was absent after the lesson there was a long silence and everyone urged each other to sustain the responsory, but everyone said that they should chant their own responsory. At last the emperor said: 'Let someone sing.' Then that downcast monk was strengthened by the will of God and encouraged by the authority he sang the responsory. Soon the most kind king, thinking that he did not know how to sing it all, ordered them to help him. When the others sang and the wretched man could not learn the verse from anyone, having sung the responsory he began to chant the Lord's Prayer in an elaborate way. All the others wanted to stop him, but the most wise Charles, wanting to find out how far he would go, forbade anyone to trouble him. He finished the verse with these words, *Adveniat regnum tuum*, and whether they wanted to or not they were compelled to respond *Fiat voluntas tua*.

When the early Lauds were finished, the king went back to his palace, or rather to his bedroom, to warm himself and equip himself in honour of such a great feast-day. He ordered that old servant and new singer to come into his presence. 'Who told you to chant that responsory?' he asked. 'Sire, you ordered someone to sing,' said the other, terrified. 'Well,' said the king (the emperor was called king at first), 'who showed you that verse?' Then the poor creature, inspired as it is thought by God, spoke as follows, in the fashion which inferiors then used to superiors, whether for honour, charm or flattery: 'Blessed lord, and beneficent king, as I could not find out the right verse from anyone, I thought that I should incur the anger of your majesty if I introduced anything strange. So I determined to intone something of which the last words usually come at the end of the responsories.' Then the most moderate emperor, smiling at him, announced in the presence of his nobles: 'That proud man who neither feared nor honoured God nor his special friend, so that he could not keep himself from his excess for a single night, that he might begin the responsory which as I have heard he was supposed to sing, by God's judgement and my own must lose his bishopric and you must administer it as God's gift with my approval according to the canonical and apostolic rule.'

6. When another bishop died the emperor put a young man in his place. When he left him cheerfully to go off and his servants brought his warhorse to the steps to be mounted according to his episcopal gravity, he was angry that they treated him as if he were infirm and mounted on the horse from the ground, so he could barely stay on and not fall off on the other side. The king, looking from the palace gallery,[15] ordered that he be summoned at once and spoke to him as follows: 'Good man, you are swift and agile, nimble and quick; you know that the calm of our empire is disturbed by many tumults of wars on all sides, so I need such a cleric in my retinue. So be the companion of our labours while you can mount your horse so swiftly.'

7. I forgot to talk about the arrangements for lections when I was talking about the ordering of responsories, so I shall treat it briefly here. No one in the basilica of the most learned Charles told people who was to recite the lections, no one marked the end of the passage with wax or made a mark with his fingernail. But they all took such trouble to familiarize themselves with what was to be read that when they were unexpectedly ordered to read they were found blameless by him. He indicated with his finger or his staff who he wanted to read, or if it was someone sitting far off he sent someone from his side. He indicated the end of the lection by a guttural sound. Everyone was so anxious about this so that whether it came at the end of a sentence or at the end of a clause or even at a lesser pause no one following dared to begin further back or further on, however strange the end or the beginning might seem, and in this way it happened that everyone in his palace was an excellent reader, even if they did not understand what they read. No one from outside, no one, even if he were well known, dared to enter his choir unless he could read and chant.

8. When he was journeying Charles came to a great church, and a wandering cleric, ignorant of Charles's discipline, came into the choir of his own accord and since he had never learned

anything of this sort he stood silent and confused in the middle of those who were chanting. The precentor[16] raised his stick and threatened to hit him unless he sang. Then he, not knowing what he should do or where he should turn, and not daring to go out, turned his neck in a circle and opened his mouth wide and tried to imitate the behaviour of someone singing as best he could. All the others could not hold back their laughter, so the very strong emperor, who could not be moved from his calm even by great events, as if he had not noticed him, waited for the end of the Mass. Then he called the poor man to him and taking pity on his efforts and strains he consoled him with these words: 'Thank you very much for your singing and your efforts, good cleric,' and he ordered that he be given a pound of silver to relieve his poverty. So that I do not seem forgetful or neglectful I record this about Alcuin's industry and his achievements, since none of his disciples failed to distinguish himself as a most holy abbot or a most holy bishop. My master G.[17] was taught the liberal arts by him, first in Gaul and later in Italy. But lest I should be accused, by those who know about these things, of a lie because I excepted no one, there were two millers' sons in his school from the monastery of St Columbanus whom it was not appropriate to raise to rule bishoprics or monasteries, but because of the merits of their teacher one after the other they most vigorously governed as stewards of the monastery of Bobbio.

9. In this way the most famous Charles, seeing the study of letters flourishing throughout all his kingdom, but lamenting that it did not reach the ripeness of the earlier fathers, though he was striving more than was human, burst out in disgust: 'Oh, if only I could have twelve clerics as learned as Jerome and Augustine were.' To which the most learned Alcuin, rightly thinking himself most unlearned in comparison to those two, full of great anger but scarcely showing it, dared to do what no other mortal would do in the sight of the dread Charles, replied: 'The creator of heaven and earth did not have many like those men, and you want to have twelve?'

10. It seems worth this matter recording here, although the people of our times will find it hard to believe, since I myself

who am writing, because of the very great difference between our chant and that of the Romans, scarcely believe it myself, except that the truth of the fathers is more to be believed than our modern lazy falsehood. Charles the tireless lover of divine service prided himself that he had done as much as was possible in the study of letters but lamented that all his provinces and regions and cities differed from one another in divine worship, that is, in the modulation of chant. He therefore asked Pope Stephen[18] of blessed memory, who, after Childeric, the most cowardly king of the Franks, had been deposed and tonsured, had anointed him as ruler of the kingdom according to the ancestral custom of the people, to send him some clerics most skilled in divine songs. He agreed to the request and the concern, which were divinely inspired, and sent twelve clerics most learned in chant, like the number of the twelve apostles, to him in Francia. When I say Francia, I mean all the provinces beyond the Alps, for as it is written: 'In those days ten men shall take hold out of all the languages of the nations, shall even take hold of the skirt of him that is a Jew,'[19] so at that time, because of the superiority of the most famous Charles, the Gauls, the Aquitanians, the Aedui, the Spaniards, the Alemannians and the Bavarians all prided themselves not a little if they earned the right to be called servants of the Franks. So when the aforementioned clerics were leaving Rome, being like all Greeks and Romans always full of envy of the fame of the Franks, they deliberated among themselves how they could vary the chant so that unity and harmony would never rejoice in his kingdom. So, coming to Charles they were received with honour and dispatched to the most prominent places. And thereupon each in his separate place began to chant as differently as possible, and to teach others to sing in like fashion, and in as false a manner as they could invent. But as the most clever Charles celebrated one year the feast of the birth and coming of Christ at the town of Trier or Metz, and most attentively and cleverly grasped and understood the style of the singing; and then the next year passed the same festivals at Paris or Tours, but hear nothing of the sound which he had experienced in the previous year; and as moreover he found that those whom he had sent into different places were also at variance with one another; so he reported the whole matter to Pope Leo, of holy memory, who had succeeded Stephen.[20] The Pope summoned the clerics back to Rome and condemned them to exile or perpetual imprisonment, and then said to the famous Charles: 'If I send you others they will be blinded with the same malice as their predecessors and will not fail to cheat you. But I think I can satisfy your wishes in this way. Send me two of the cleverest clerics that you have by you, in such a way that those who are with me may not know that they belong to you, and, with God's help, they shall attain to as perfect a knowledge of those things as you desire.'[21] And thus it was done. And after a short time the Pope sent them back, excellently trained, to Charles. One of them he kept at his own court; the other at the request of his son Drogo, bishop of Metz,[22] he sent to that church. And his activity not only showed itself to be powerful in that city, but it soon spread so widely throughout all Francia, that now all in these regions who use the Latin tongue called the ecclesiastical chant Metensian;[23] But among us, who use the Teutonic or Teuthiscan tongue, it is called in the vernacular Met or Mette; or if the Greek derivation is used it is called Mettisc.[24]

11. It was the habit of the most religious and moderate Charles to take food during Lent at the eighth hour of the day after Mass and evening Lauds had been celebrated: and in so doing he was not breaking the fast, for he was following the Lord's command in taking food at an earlier hour than usual.[25] Now a certain bishop, who offended against the maxim of the wise man in being very just but particularly foolish,[26] unwisely criticized him for this. Whereupon the most wise Charles concealed his wrath, and humbly received the bishop's admonition, saying: 'Good bishop, your admonition is good; but now I command you that you should take no food until the very humblest of my servants, who are in my court, have been fed.' Now while Charles was eating he was waited upon by magnates and tyrants and kings of various peoples; and when his banquet was ended, those who served him fed and they were served by counts and prefects and nobles of various ranks. And when

these last had made an end of eating then came the military officers and the scholars of the palace: then the chiefs of the various departments of the palace; then their subordinates, then the servants of those servants, so that the last comers did not eat before the middle of the night. When therefore Lent was nearly ended, and the bishop in question had endured this punishment all the time, the most merciful Charles said to him: 'Now, bishop, I think you have found out that it is not lack of self-restraint but care for others which makes me dine in Lent before the hour of evening.'

12. Once he asked another bishop for his blessing and he thereupon, after blessing the bread, first took some for himself and then wanted to pass it to the most honourable Charles; who, however, said to him: 'You may keep all the bread for yourself'; and thus, much to the bishop's confusion, he refused to receive his blessing.

13. The most careful Charles would never give more than one county to any of his counts unless they happened to live on the borders or marches of the barbarians; nor would he ever give a bishop any abbacy or churches that were in the royal gift unless there were very special reasons for doing it. When his councillors or friends asked him why he did this, he would answer: 'With that estate or that, with that little abbey or that church I can secure the fidelity of some vassal, as good a man as any bishop or count, and perhaps better.' But when there were special reasons he would give several benefices to one man; as he did for instance to Udalric,[27] brother of the great Hildegard, mother of kings and emperors. Now Udalric, after Hildegard's death, was deprived of his honours for a certain offence; and a jester thereupon said in the hearing of the most merciful Charles: 'Now has Udalric, by the death of his sister, lost all his honours in both east and west.' Charles, moved to tears by these words, restored to him at once all his former honours. When justice bade him, he opened his hands, most widely and liberally, to certain holy places, as will appear in what follows.

14. There was a certain bishopric which lay right in Charles's path when he journeyed, and which indeed he could hardly

avoid. The bishop of this place, always anxious to give satis-
faction, put everything that he had at Charles's disposal. But
on one occasion the emperor arrived unexpectedly, and then
the bishop in great anxiety had to fly hither and thither like a
swallow, and had not only the churches and the houses but also
the courts and squares swept and cleaned: and then, tired and
irritated, came to meet him. The most pious Charles noticed
this, and looked carefully around and examined all the details.
Then he said to the bishop: 'My kind host, you always have
everything splendidly cleaned for my arrival.' Then the bishop,
as if divinely inspired, bowed low and grasped the king's never-
conquered right hand, and hiding his irritation as best he could,
kissed it and said: 'It is but right, my lord, that, wherever you
come, all things should be thoroughly cleansed.' Then Charles,
of all kings the wisest, understanding the state of affairs said to
him: 'If I empty I can also fill.' And he added: 'You may have
that estate which lies close to your bishopric, and all your
successors may have it until the end of time.'

15. On that same journey he came unexpectedly to a bishop
who lived in a place through which he had to pass. Now on
that day, being the sixth day of the week, he was not willing to
eat the flesh of beast or bird; and the bishop, being by reason
of the nature of the place unable to procure fish quickly, ordered
some excellent cheese, rich and creamy, to be placed before
him. And the most moderate Charles, with the readiness which
he showed everywhere and on all occasions, spared the blushes
of the bishop and required nothing else: but taking up his knife
cut off the skin, which he thought unsavoury, and fell to on the
white of the cheese. Thereupon the bishop, who was standing
near like a servant, drew closer and said: 'Why do you do that,
lord emperor? You are throwing away the very best part.' Then
Charles, who deceived no one, and did not believe that anyone
would deceive him, on the persuasion of the bishop put a piece
of the skin in his mouth, and slowly ate it and swallowed it like
butter. Then approving of the advice of the bishop, he said:
'Very true, my good host,' and he added: 'Be sure to send me
at Aachen every year two cart-loads full of this sort of cheese.'
The bishop was alarmed at the impossibility of the task and,

fearful of losing both his rank and his office, he rejoined: 'My lord, I can procure the cheeses, but I cannot tell which are of this quality and which of another. Much I fear lest I fall under your censure.' Then Charles, from whose penetration and skill nothing could escape, however new or strange it might be, spoke thus to the bishop, who from childhood had known such cheeses and yet could not test them: 'Cut them in two,' he said, 'then fasten together with a skewer those that you find to be of the right quality and put them in a barrel and then send them to me. The rest you may keep for yourself and your clergy and your family.' This was done for two years and the king ordered the present of cheeses to be taken in without comment: then in the third year the bishop brought in person his laboriously collected cheeses. But the most just Charles pitied his labour and anxiety and added to the bishopric an excellent estate whence he and his successors might provide themselves with corn and wine.

16. As we have shown how the most wise Charles exalted the humble, let us now show how he brought low the proud. There was a bishop who was extremely greedy for fame and foolish things. The most shrewd Charles heard of this and told a certain Jewish merchant, whose custom it was to go to the promised land and bring from thence rare and wonderful things to the countries beyond the sea, to deceive or cheat this bishop in whatever way he could. So the Jew caught an ordinary house mouse and stuffed it with various spices, and then offered it for sale to the bishop, saying that he had brought from Judaea this most precious animal, never seen before. The bishop was filled with such joy at this, and offered the Jew three pounds of silver for the precious article. Then the Jew said: 'A fine price indeed for so precious an article! I had rather throw it into the depths of the sea than let any man have it at so cheap and shameful a price.' So the bishop, who had much wealth and never gave anything to the poor, offered him ten pounds of silver for the incomparable treasure. But the cunning man, with pretended indignation, replied: 'The God of Abraham forbid that I should thus lose the fruit of my labour and transport.' Then the greedy cleric, all eager for the prize, offered him twenty pounds. But

the Jew in high dudgeon wrapped up the mouse in the most costly silk and began to leave. Then the bishop, as thoroughly taken in as he deserved to be, offered a full measure of silver to obtain the priceless object. And so at last the merchant yielded to his entreaties with much show of reluctance: and, taking the silver went to the emperor and told him everything. After a few days the king called together all the bishops and nobles of that province to his assembly; and, after many needful matters had been considered, he ordered all that silver to be brought and placed in the middle of the palace. Then thus he spoke and said: 'Fathers and guardians, bishops of our Church, you ought to minister to the poor, or rather to Christ in them, and not to seek after vanities. But now you act quite contrary to this; and are vainglorious[28] and avaricious beyond all other men.' Then he added: 'One of you has given a Jew all this silver for a painted mouse.' Then the bishop who had been so wickedly deceived threw himself at Charles's feet and begged pardon for his sin. Charles upbraided him in suitable words and then allowed him to depart in confusion.

17. This same bishop was left to take care of the most renowned Hildegard, when the most warlike Charles was engaged in campaigns against the Avars. When he began to be excited by his intimacy with her he had the audacity to ask her to allow him to use the golden sceptre of the incomparable Charles on festal days instead of his episcopal staff. She deceived him cleverly, and said that she dare not give it to anyone, but that she would carry his request faithfully to the king. When Charles came back, she jestingly told him of the request of the mad bishop. He kindly promised to do what she wished and even more. When almost all Europe had come together to greet Charles after his victory over so mighty a people, he pronounced these words in the hearing of small and great: 'Bishops should despise this world and inspire others by their example to seek after heavenly things. But now they are corrupted by ambition beyond all the rest of mankind; and one of them not content with holding the first episcopal see in Germany has dared without my approval to claim my golden sceptre, which I carry to signify my royal will, in order that he might use it as his pastoral

staff.' The guilty man acknowledged his sin, received pardon
and retired.

18. Now, my lord emperor Charles,[29] I much fear that
through my desire to obey your orders I may incur the enmity
of all who have taken vows and especially of the highest clergy
of all. But for all this I do not greatly care, if only I be not
deprived of your protection. The most religious emperor
Charles gave orders that all bishops throughout his wide kingdom should preach in their cathedral before a certain day,
which he appointed, under penalty of being deprived of the
episcopal dignity if they failed to comply with the order. But
why do I say 'dignity' when the Apostle protests: 'He that
desires the office of a bishopric desires a good work'?[30] But in
truth I must confess to you that there is great 'dignity' in
the office, but there is no less need of 'good work'. Well, the
aforementioned bishop was at first alarmed at this command,
because gluttony and pride were all his learning, and he feared
that if he lost his bishopric he would lose his luxury at the same
time. So he invited two of the palace nobles on the festal day,
and after the reading of the Gospel mounted the pulpit as
though he were going to address the people. All the people ran
together in wonder at so unexpected an occurrence, except one
poor red-headed fellow, who had his head covered with his
boot because he had no hat and was foolishly ashamed of his
red hair. Then the bishop – bishop in name but not in deed –
called to his doorkeeper, or rather his henchman (whose dignity
and duties went by the name of the aedileship among the ancient
Romans), and said: 'Bring me that man in the hat who is
standing there near the door of the church.' The doorkeeper
made haste to obey, seized the poor man and began to drag
him towards the bishop. But he feared some heavy penalty for
daring to stand in the house of God with covered head, and
struggled with all his might to avoid being brought before the
tribunal of the most harsh judge. But the bishop, looking from
his perch, now addressing his vassal and now chiding the poor
knave, bawled out and preached as follows: 'Here with him!
Willy-nilly you've got to come.' When at last force or fear
brought him near, the bishop cried: 'Come nearer; you must

come quite close.' Then he snatched the head-covering from his
captive and cried to the people: 'Lo and behold, all ye people:
this lazy fellow is red-headed.' Then he returned to the altar
and performed the ceremony, or pretended to perform it. When
the Mass was brought to an end his guests passed into his hall,
which was decorated with many-coloured carpets and cloths of
all kinds; and there a sumptuous banquet, served in gold and
silver and jewelled cups, was provided, calculated to tickle the
appetite of the fastidious or the well fed. The bishop himself
sat on the softest of cushions, clad in precious silks and wearing
the imperial purple, so that he seemed a king except for the
sceptre and the title. He was surrounded by troops of rich
soldiers, in comparison with whom the officers of the palace
(nobles though they were) of the unconquered Charles seemed
to themselves most mean. When they asked leave to depart
after this wonderful and more than royal banquet he, desiring to
show still more plainly his magnificence and his glory, ordered
masters most skilled in singing to come forward, with all kinds
of musical instruments, the sound of whose voices could soften
the hardest hearts or turn to ice the swiftly flowing waters of
the Rhine. And at the same time every kind of choice drink,
subtly and variously compounded with various spices and
drugs, was offered them in bowls garlanded with herbs and
flowers, pouring their sheen on the gold and gems with which
they were decorated: but their stomachs could contain no more
and so the drinks lay idle in their hands. Meanwhile bakers and
butchers, cooks and sausage-makers, offered preparations of
exquisite art to stimulate their appetite, though their stomachs
could contain no more: it was a banquet such as was never
offered even to the great Charles himself.

When morning came and the bishop returned some way
towards soberness, he thought with fear of the luxury he had
paraded before the servants of the emperor. So he called them
into his presence, loaded them with presents worthy of a king
and implored them to speak to the dread Charles of the goodness and simplicity of his life; and above all to tell him how he
had preached publicly before them in his cathedral.

Upon their return, Charles asked them why the bishop had

invited them. Thereupon they fell at his feet and said: 'Master, it was that he might honour us in your name, far beyond our humble deserts.' 'He is', they went on, 'in every way most faithful to you and the best of bishops and most worthy of the highest rank in the Church. For, if you will trust our poor judgement, we profess to your sublime majesty that we heard him preach in his church in the most rhetorical fashion.' Then the emperor, who knew the bishop's lack of skill, pressed them further as to the manner of his preaching; and they dared not deceive him but told everything as it had happened. Then the emperor saw that he had made an effort to say something rather than disobey the imperial order; and he allowed him, in spite of his unworthiness, to retain the bishopric.

19. Shortly after, a young man, a relation of the king's, sang, on the occasion of some festival, the Alleluia admirably: and the emperor turned to this same bishop and said: 'My cleric is singing very well.' But the stupid man thought that he was jesting and did not know that the cleric was the emperor's relation; and so he answered: 'Any clown in our countryside drones as well as that to his oxen at their ploughing.' At this most unsuitable answer the emperor turned on him the lightning of his flashing eyes and dashed him terror-stricken to the very ground.

20. There was another bishop in a very tiny little city who while he was alive did not want to be seen like the apostles and martyrs as an intercessor to God, but wanted to be worshipped with divine honours. But he tried to conceal such pride in this way, so that he would be called a holy man of God and not thought by everyone to be deserving of abhorrence like pagan idols. He had a vassal, not without rank among the citizens, very eager and hard-working. The bishop never gave him any gift or even any kind word. He, not knowing what he could do to please his harsh mind, thought that if he said he had done some miracle in his name he might be worthy to come to his favour. So when he decided to go from his house to the bishop he took two small dogs with him, which in the French language are called *veltres*, which are so swift that they can easily catch foxes and other small animals, and what is more they could

easily take quails and other birds which are flushed out quickly, and when he saw a fox stalking the mice he suddenly set the dogs on it without a word. Dashing after it most swiftly they caught it a bowshot away. He followed their tracks and snatched it alive and well from the teeth and jaws of the dogs. Then, having hidden the dogs where he could, he went to his master with the spoils and humbly began: 'See, master, what kind of gift a poor man like me has been able to get.' Then the bishop, smiling a little, asked how he had caught it so unharmed. And he, going closer and swearing by the life of his master that he would not conceal the truth from him, said: 'Master, I was riding through this field and saw this fox not far off and, slackening the reins, I started after him. And when he fled so quickly that I could barely see him, I raised my hand and conjured him saying "In the name of my master Recho,[31] stay still and don't move." And as if he was bound in chains he stayed fixed to the spot until I picked him up like a lost sheep.' Then he, puffed up with a foolish gesture, said to everyone: 'Now my sanctity is clear, now I know who I am, now I recognize what I shall be.' And from that day he treated that hated man with a special love more than any of his household.

21. Because the opportunity has offered itself, even though they are not related to the subject, I want to record other matters which happened at the same time and are worthy of being remembered. There was a certain bishop in East Francia,[32] of wonderful holiness and abstinence, of incomparable generosity and compassion. The old enemy, envious of his goodness as of all justice, aroused in him so great a desire to eat meat in Lent that he thought he would die without delay unless he could be restored by this sort of food. The bishop was reassured by the advice of many holy and venerable priests that he should take meat to restore his strength and that afterwards he could fast, as was his custom, for the rest of the year. So that he should not be found disobedient to them and be the destroyer of his own life he yielded to their authority, driven by ultimate necessity, and he put a little animal flesh into his mouth. When he began to chew it and to savour its taste a very little on his palate he felt such great dislike, disgust and hatred not only for

meat and for all kinds of food but even for daylight and for life
and he was so overcome by despair for his own salvation that
he did not want to eat or drink any longer or to place his hope
in the saviour of sinners. As the first week of Lent passed, the
fathers I have mentioned suggested to him that, as he was aware
that he was deceived by an illusion from the devil, he should
try to vanquish, mitigate or wash away his brief sin by means
of even harsher fasts and contrition of heart and generous
almsgiving. He obeyed their advice, since he was very well
taught, so that he could both confound the wickedness of the
devil and seek forgiveness for what he had done from the
restorer of innocence, inflicting on himself two- and even three-
day fasts, abandoning the rest of sleep; and he himself minis-
tered every day to the poor and to pilgrims, washing their feet
and offering them clothes and money as best he could and
wanting to give even more. On the holy day of Easter Saturday
he asked for many large jars from the whole city and took care
to offer warm baths from morning to evening to all who wanted
them. With his own hand he shaved everyone's necks and with
his nails he removed purulent scabs from their hairy bodies and
anointed them with unguents and dressed them in white robes
as a sign of their rebirth. When the sun was about to set and
there was no one left who had not undergone such ministrations
he himself went into the bath and came out with a clear conscience and put on the cleanest linen garments, so that with the
approval of the holy bishops he might celebrate the feast with
the people. When he was going to the church the cunning
enemy, who wanted to do violence to his plan and had left
one poor man unwashed, contrary to his vow, assumed the
appearance of a very filthy and very ghastly leper with running
pus and in rags stiff with putrid gore and with tottering step
and the voice of someone hoarse, and he met him in front of
the entrance to the church. Then the holy bishop turned back,
inspired by heaven so that he recognized the enemy whose
victim he had lately been. He took off his garments, ordered
more water to be heated without delay and had the wretch put
into it. Then he seized a razor and began to shave his most
filthy neck. When he had shaved from one ear to the middle of

the windpipe he started at the other ear so he might get to the middle, but when he got there he found that the long bristles he had previously shaved off had grown again. And when this had happened often, and he did not stop shaving, behold in the hands of the bishop a huge eye began to appear in the centre of the windpipe which I shudder to describe.[33] The bishop, terrified, leaped back from such a dreadful sight and with a great cry crossed himself in the name of Christ. Before Christ had been invoked the deceitful enemy, unable to hide his deception any longer, vanished like smoke, and as he went he said: 'This eye was watching carefully when you ate meat in Lent.'

22. In the same region there was another bishop who was of incomparable holiness. With incautious freedom from care, as one almost ignorant of the female sex, he permitted young nuns as well as older priests to associate with him in order to learn. During the feast of Easter, after the divine office, which lasted until after the middle of the night, he indulged himself freely in the Alsatian wine from Sigolsheim[34] as well as a stronger Falernian. All too excited, he enticed a certain most beautiful woman with the moves of a harlot, and when the others had left he called her to his bed and, disastrously, he had intercourse with her. When dawn broke he got up quickly and like the pagans he washed the night away[35] and with a stained conscience went before the eyes of the true God, whom no one can escape. When the first music was over, according to his office he had to begin the angelic hymn, he was terrified and remained silent, and laying the vestments of his holy office upon the altar he turned to the people and confessed his sin. Then rushing to the foot of the altar he burst into floods of tears. The people insisted that he should get up and with terrible oaths they insisted that on that special day they would not let anyone celebrate Masses for them except their bishop. And he could not move from the spot, and this dispute continued for almost three hours. At last, the mercy of the Creator taking pity on the vows of the faithful people and the contrite heart of the bishop, he was dressed again in his vestments as he lay on the floor and, assured of God's indulgence, he was raised up to perform the fearful mysteries in the model of a true penitent, or as a warning

that in this world safety is never sure but always and everywhere groundless.

23. In what is called Old Francia there was another bishop who was fettered by extreme greed. When one year the failure of all of the crops ravaged the whole world, that miserly trader rejoiced that everyone was near to death and in extreme need, and he ordered his storehouses to be opened so that goods might be sold far too dearly. Then a demon or hobgoblin[36] whose function was to spend time on games and in deceiving men had the habit of coming to the house of a blacksmith and spending the night playing with his hammers and anvils. When the master of the house tried to protect himself and his possessions with the sign of the holy Cross, the hairy creature replied: 'If you don't stop me playing in your shop, mate, bring your tankard here and you will find it full every day.' The poor man was more afraid of bodily hunger than of the eternal damnation of his soul and he did what his enemy had persuaded him to. Taking a huge flask, and repeatedly breaking into the cellar of his Bromius or Dis,[37] and after his theft he let the remainder flow all over the floor. And when in this way a great many barrels had been emptied the bishop thought that they had been wasted by a trick of demons. He sprinkled the room with holy water and protected it with the sign of the invincible Cross. When night fell the cunning servant of the ancient thief came along with his flask and when he did not dare to touch the wine jars because of the mark of the holy Cross, and was not able to get out, he was found in human form and tied up by the watchman of the house. He was led before the people as a thief and publicly flogged. As he was being beaten he said: 'Woe is me, woe is me, for I have lost my mate's tankard.' I tell this story here, although the tale is true, so that it may be known who benefits from things abjured and hidden in the day of need, and how great is the power of the invocation of the holy name, even if used by the wicked.

24. While I turn my gaze on the head of the Franks and go through its limbs, I have left behind the other nations, great and small. But now I come to our neighbours, the Italians, who are separated from us by a single barrier. There was there a

bishop who was extremely greedy for frightful things. The Devil noticed this and appeared in human form to a poor man who was not free from greed, and promised him that he would make him very rich if he would bind himself to him for ever. When the wretch did not shrink from profiting from this, the cunning enemy said: 'I will turn myself into a most excellent mule, you will climb on my back and ride to the bishop's court. When he begins to gaze eagerly at the mule you drag the matter out, delay, reject his price, exaggerate your anger and pretend you are ready to leave. Then he will have to come after you and promise more. At last give in to his pleas and having heaped up a vast amount of money let him have the mule as if forced to it against your will, and go forth in haste find a hiding-place somewhere.' All this was done and the bishop could not wait until the next day but mounted his steed in the midday sun, riding through the town to show it off. He galloped off into the open fields and hastened to a river to cool down. Everyone followed, watching its whirling, its running at full speed and its swimming like a dolphin. And behold, the old Belial, not enduring spur or rein, and sweating with the fires of hell, plunged into the depths of the abyss and began to drag the bishop in with him. He could scarcely be pulled out by the effort of a band of soldiers and fishermen who were sailing close by.

25. The enemy skilled in ambushes, accustomed to laying a snare in the way that we walk,[38] does not cease to overthrow us in one way or another by some fault or other. A certain priest (the bishop's name must be concealed in such a case) was accused of the crime of fornication. When this came to the notice of the people and was brought to the attention of the most famous Charles, the bishop of bishops and that wisest of men did not want to give faith to idle words and so concealed the matter for some time, but rumour, of all evils the most swift,[39] starting small as a tomtit exceeds the size of eagles, so that it can never be hidden. Charles, that most rigorous seeker after justice, sent two of his courtiers, who were to turn aside that evening to a place near the city and early in the morning to come to the bishop unexpectedly and ask him to celebrate a Mass for them. If he should refuse, they should compel him in

his own name to celebrate the holy mysteries in person. Not knowing what he should do, since he had sinned that night before the eyes of the heavenly judge, and not daring to offend them, but fearing men more than God, he bathed his burning limbs in the coldest spring and went forth to offer the awesome sacraments. And behold, either conscience gripped his heart or the water penetrated his veins, for he was seized with such icy cold that no doctor had any remedy to help him, and by a most cruel attack of fever he was led to death and compelled to surrender his soul to the decree of the strict and eternal judge.

26. Though through these and similar tricks other mortals are deceived by the Devil and his attendants we should look at the saying of the Lord, rewarding the most strong confession of St Peter: 'Thou art Peter, and upon this rock I will build my Church, and the gates of hell shall not prevail against it'[40] and it shall remain unshaken and unmoved in these most dangerous and most wicked times. Among rivals, envy always rages and so it was the solemn custom of the Romans that they were all hostile or rather violent to anyone of any importance ever raised to the apostolic seat. Thus it happened that some of them, blinded by envy, accused the above-mentioned Pope Leo, of blessed memory, of a deadly crime and then tried to put out his eyes. But they were frightened and held back by some divine impulse, and did not put out his eyes but slashed him with their knives. He secretly sent the news of this to Michael, emperor of Constantinople, and he withheld any help for him, saying: 'The pope has his own realm and it is greater than ours. He himself must take revenge on his enemies.' Then the holy man, following the divine plan, asked the unconquered Charles to come to Rome, and since he was already ruler and emperor of many nations, to receive now the name of Emperor, Caesar and Augustus by apostolic authority.

Now Charles was always ready to march and, in warlike array, though he knew nothing at all of the cause of the summons, came at once with his attendants and the troop of his young soldiers; the head of the world came to the city that had once been the head of the world. And when the most corrupt people heard of his sudden coming, at once, just as sparrows hide themselves when they hear the voice of their master, so they fled and hid in various hiding-places, cellars and refuges. Nowhere under heaven, however, could they escape from his energy and penetration; and soon they were captured and brought in chains to the basilica of St Peter. Then the undaunted father Leo took the Gospel of our Lord Jesus Christ and held it over his head, and then in the presence of Charles and his soldiers, with his persecutors standing round, he swore in the following words: 'Just as on the day of the great judgement I may partake in the Gospel, so I am innocent of the charge that is falsely laid against me.'[41] Then the dread Charles said to his servants: 'Take care that none of them escapes.' Then he condemned all who had been taken prisoner either to some kind of death or to perpetual banishment.[42]

As Charles stayed in Rome for a few days for the sake of the army, the bishop of the apostolic see called together all who were able to come from the neighbouring districts and then, in their presence and in the presence of all the counts of the unconquered Charles, he declared him to be Emperor and Defender of the Roman Church. Now Charles had no guess of what was coming; and, though he could not refuse what seemed to have been divinely preordained for him, nevertheless he received his new title with no show of thankfulness. For first he thought that the Greeks would be fired by greater envy than ever and would plan some harm against the kingdom of the Franks; or at least would take greater precautions against a possible sudden attack of Charles to subdue their kingdom and add it to his own empire. And further, the magnanimous Charles recalled how ambassadors from the king of Constantinople had come to him and had told him that their master wished to be his loyal friend; and that, if they became nearer neighbours, he had determined to treat him as his son and relieve the poverty of Charles from his resources: and how, upon hearing this, Charles had been unable to contain any longer the most fervent fire of his heart and had exclaimed: 'Oh, would that that pool were not between us; for then we would either divide between us the wealth of the East, or we would hold it in common.' Ignoring the poverty of Africa, they used to tell this story about the king of the Africans.

But the Lord, who is both the giver and the restorer of health, so showed his favour to the innocence of the blessed Leo that he restored his eyes to be brighter than they were before that wicked and cruel cutting; except only that, in token of his virtue, a most beautiful scar (like a very fine thread) marked his eyelids.

27. The foolish may accuse me of folly because just now I made Charles say that the sea, which that mighty emperor called playfully a little pool, lay between us and the Greeks; but I must tell my critics that at that date the Avars and the Bulgars and many other powerful races barred the way to Greece with forces yet unattacked and unbroken. Soon afterwards, it is true, the most warlike Charles either hurled them to the ground, as he did the Slavs and the Bulgars; or else utterly destroyed them, as was the case with the Avars, that race of iron and diamond. And I will go on to speak of these exploits as soon as I have said a few words about the wonderful buildings which Charles (Emperor, Augustus and Caesar), following the example of the all-wise Solomon, built at Aachen, either for God, or for himself, or for the bishops, abbots, counts and all guests that came to him from all quarters of the world.

28. When the most energetic emperor Charles was able to have some rest he did not seek sluggish ease, but wanted to toil in the service of God. He desired therefore to build upon his native soil a basilica finer even than the ancient buildings of the Romans, and soon his purpose was realized. To build it he summoned architects and skilled workmen from all lands beyond the seas; and above all he placed a certain very skilled abbot whose competence for the execution of such tasks he knew, though he knew not of his crimes. When the Augustus had gone on a certain journey, this abbot allowed anyone to depart home who would pay sufficient money: and those who could not purchase their discharge, or were not allowed to return by their masters, he burdened with unending labours, as the Egyptians once afflicted the people of God.[43] By such deceitfulness he gathered together a great mass of gold and

silver and silken robes; and exhibiting in his chamber only the least precious articles, he concealed in boxes and chests all the richest treasures. One day there was brought to him on a sudden the news that his house was on fire. He ran, in great excitement, and pushed his way through the mass of flames[44] into the locked room where his boxes, stuffed with gold, were kept: he was not satisfied to take one away, but would only leave after he had loaded his servants with a box apiece on their shoulders. And as he was going out a huge beam, dislodged by the fire, fell on top of him; and then his body was burned by temporal flames and his soul was sent to the flames which are not quenched. Thus did the judgement of God keep watch for the most religious emperor Charles, when his attention was withdrawn by the business of his kingdom.

29. There was another workman, the most skilled of all in every kind of working in bronze and glass. Now this man (his name was Tanco and he was at one time a monk of St Gall) cast a fine bell and the emperor was delighted with its sound. Then said that most distinguished, but most unfortunate worker in brass: 'Lord emperor, give orders that a great weight of copper be brought to me that I may refine it; and instead of tin give me as much silver as I shall need – a hundred pounds at least; and I will cast such a bell for you that this will seem dumb in comparison to it.' Then Charles, the most liberal of monarchs, who 'if riches increase set not his heart upon them',[45] readily gave the necessary orders. He took it and went off rejoicing, he smelted and refined the brass; but he used, not silver, but the purest sort of tin, and soon he made a bell, much better than the one that the emperor had formerly admired, and, when he had tested it, he took it to the emperor, who admired its exquisite shape and ordered an iron clapper to be inserted and the bell to be hung in the bell-tower. That was soon done; and then the warden of the church, the attendants and even the boys of the place tried, one after the other, to make the bell sound. But all was in vain; and so at last the knavish maker of the bell came up, seized the rope, and pulled at the bell. And behold the iron fell out of the middle, right on the head of the cheating brass founder, killed him on the spot

and passed straight through his carcass and crashed to the ground, carrying his bowels and genitals with it. When the aforementioned weight of silver was found, the most righteous Charles ordered it to be distributed among the poorest servants of the palace.

30. Now it was a rule at that time that if the imperial mandate had gone out that any task was to be accomplished, whether it was the making of bridges or ships or causeways, or the cleansing or paving or filling up of muddy roads, the counts might execute the less important work through the agency of their deputies or servants; but for the greater enterprises, and especially such as were of an original kind, no duke or count, no bishop or abbot could possibly get himself excused. The arches of the great bridge at Mainz bear witness to this; for all Europe, so to speak, laboured at this work in a most orderly co-operation, and then the knavery of a few rascals, who wanted to steal merchandise from the ships that passed underneath, destroyed it.[46] If any churches which belonged to the king wanted decorating with carved ceilings or wall paintings, the neighbouring bishops and abbots had to take charge of the task; but if new churches had to be built then all bishops, dukes and counts, all abbots and heads of royal churches and all who were in occupation of any public office had to work at it with never-ceasing labour from its foundations to its roof. You may see the proof of the emperor's skill in the divine and human basilica at Aachen, you may see it in the houses of all ranks of men which, by Charles's device, were built round his own palace in such a way that from the windows of his chamber he could see all who went out or came in and what they were doing, while they believed themselves free from observation;[47] you may see it in all the houses of his nobles, which were lifted up on high from the ground in such a fashion that beneath them the retainers of his nobles and the servants of those retainers and every class of man could be protected from rain or snow, from cold or heat, while at the same time they were not concealed from the eyes of the most vigilant Charles. But I am a prisoner within my monastery walls and your court officials are free; and I will therefore leave to them the task of describing the

cathedral, while I return to speak of how the judgement of God was made manifest in the building of it.

31. The most careful Charles ordered certain nobles of the neighbourhood to support with all their power the workmen whom he had set to their task, and to supply everything they required for it. Those workmen who came from a distance he gave in charge to a certain Liutfrid, the steward of his palace, telling him to feed and clothe them at the public expense and also most carefully to provide anything that was wanting for the building. The steward obeyed these commands for the short time that Charles remained in that place; but after his departure neglected them altogether, and by cruel tortures collected such a mass of money from the poor workmen that Pluto and Dis would not be able to carry their wealth to hell except on a camel. Now this was found out in the following way. The most glorious Charles used to go to Lauds at night in a long and flowing cloak, of a kind which is now neither used nor known: then when the morning hymns were over he would go back to his chamber and dress himself in his imperial robes. All the clerics used to come ready robed to the nightly office, and then they would wait for the emperor to go to Mass, either in the church or in the porch which was then called the outer court. Sometimes they would remain awake, or if anyone had need of sleep he would lean his head for a little while on his companion's breast. Now one poor cleric, who used often to go to Liutfrid's house to get his clothes (rags, I ought to call them) washed and mended, was sleeping with his head on a friend's knees, when he saw in a vision a giant, taller than the adversary of St Anthony,[48] come from the king's court and hurry, over the bridge that spanned a little stream, to the house of the steward; and he led with him an enormous camel, burdened with baggage of inestimable value. In his dream, he was struck with amazement and he asked the giant who he was and whither he wished to go. And the giant answered: 'I come from the house of the king and I go to the house of Liutfrid; and I shall place Liutfrid on these packages and I shall take him and them down with me to hell.'

Thereupon the cleric woke up, in a fright lest the most dread

Charles should find him sleeping. He lifted up his head and urged the others to wakefulness and cried: 'Hear, I pray you, my dream. I seemed to see another Polyphemus,[49] who walked on the earth and yet touched the stars, and passed through the Ionian Sea without wetting his sides. I saw him hasten from the royal court to the house of Liutfrid with a laden camel. And when I asked the cause of his journey, he said: "I am going to put Liutfrid on the top of the load, and then take him to hell."'

The story was hardly finished when there came from his house a girl known to everyone, who fell at their feet and asked them to remember her friend Liutfrid in their prayers. And, when they asked the reason for her words, she said: 'My lords, he went out to the lavatory in good health, and, as he stayed a long time, we went in search of him, and found him dead.' When the emperor heard of his sudden death, and was informed by the workmen and his servants of his grasping avarice, he ordered his treasures to be examined. They were found to be of priceless worth, and when the emperor, after God the greatest of judges, found by what wickedness they had been collected he gave this public judgement: 'Nothing of that which was gained by fraud can go to the liberation of his soul. Let his wealth be divided among the workmen of this our building, and the poorer servants of our palace.'

32. Now I must speak of two things which happened in that same place. There was a deacon who followed the custom of those beyond the Alps and resisted the course of nature. For he went to the baths and had himself closely shaved, polished his skin, cleaned his nails, and had his hair cut very short as if it had been done by a lathe. Then he put on linen undergarments and a very white shirt, and then, because he must not miss his turn, or rather desiring to make a fine show, he proceeded to read the Gospel before God and His holy angels, and in the presence of the most watchful king; his heart in the meantime being unclean, as events were to show. For while he was reading, a spider came down from the ceiling by a thread, hooked itself on to the deacon's head, and then ran up again. The most observant Charles saw this happen a second and a third time, but pretended not to notice it, and the cleric, because of the

emperor's presence, dare not keep the spider off with his hand, and moreover did not know that it was a spider attacking him, but thought that he was being tickled by flies. So he finished the reading of the Gospel, and also went through the rest of the office. But when he left the cathedral he soon began to swell up, and died within an hour. But the most devout Charles, inasmuch as he had seen his danger and had not prevented it, thought himself guilty of manslaughter and did public penance.[50]

33. Now the most glorious Charles had a certain cleric who was unsurpassed in every respect. And of him that was said which was never said of any other mortal man: for it was said that he excelled all mankind in knowledge of both sacred and profane literature; in ecclesiastical chant and popular song in the composition and modulation of poems and in the sweetest fullness of his voice and in the incredible pleasure which he gave. Other men have had drawbacks to compensate for their excellences; for Moses the lawgiver, filled with wisdom by the teaching of God, nevertheless complains that 'he is not eloquent' but 'slow of speech, and of a slow tongue',[51] and sent therefore Joshua to take counsel with Eleazar, the high priest, who by authority of God, who dwelt within him, commanded even the heavenly bodies: and Christ our Lord did not allow John the Baptist to work any miracle while in the body, though he bore witness that 'among them that are born of women there hath not arisen a greater' than he:[52] and He bade Peter revere the wisdom of Paul, though Peter by the revelation of the Father recognized Him and received from Him the keys of the kingdom of heaven: and He allowed John, the disciple He loved best, to fall into so great a terror that he did not dare to come into the place of His sepulchre, though weak women paid many visits to it.[53]

But as the Scriptures say: 'Unto everyone that hath shall be given';[54] and those, who know from whom they have the little which they possess, succeed; while he who knows not the giver of his possessions, or, if he knows it, gives not due thanks to the giver, loses everything. For, while this wonderful cleric was standing like one of his intimates near the most glorious

emperor, suddenly he disappeared. The unconquered emperor
Charles was dumbfounded at so unheard of and incredible an
occurrence: but, after he had made the sign of the cross, he
found in the place where the cleric had stood something that
seemed to be a foul-smelling coal, which had just ceased to
burn.

34. The mention of the trailing garment that the emperor
wore at night has diverted us from his military array. Now the
dress and equipment of the old Franks was as follows. Their
boots were gilt on the outside and decorated with laces three
cubits long. The thongs round the legs were red, and under
them they wore upon their legs and thighs linen of the same
colour, artistically embroidered. The laces stretched above these
linen garments and above the crossed thongs, sometimes under
them and sometimes over them, now in front of the leg and
now behind. Then came a rich linen shirt and then a buckled
sword-belt. The great sword was surrounded first with a sheath,
then with a covering of leather, and lastly with a linen wrap
hardened with shining wax.

The last part of their dress was a white or blue cloak in the
shape of a double square; so that when it was placed upon the
shoulders it touched the feet in front and behind, but at the side
hardly came down to the knees. In the right hand was carried
a stick of apple-wood, with regular knots, strong and terrible;
a handle of gold or silver decorated with figures was fastened
to it. I myself am lazy and slower than a tortoise, and so
never got into Francia; but I saw the king of the Franks in the
monastery of St Gall, glittering in the dress I have described,
with two golden flowers springing from his thighs, of which
the first was as tall as the king himself. But the second, growing
gradually upwards, adorned the top of his head with great glory
and sheltered him when he walked.

But the habits of man change; and when the Franks, in their
wars with the Gauls, saw the latter proudly wearing little striped
cloaks, they dropped their national customs and began to imitate the Gauls. At first the strictest of emperors did not forbid
the new habit, because it seemed more suitable for war: but,
when he found that the Frisians were abusing his permission,

and were selling these little cloaks at the same price as the old large ones, he gave orders that no one should buy from them, at the usual price, anything but the old cloaks, broad, wide and long: and he added: 'What is the good of those little napkins? I cannot cover myself with them in bed and when I am on horseback I cannot shield myself with them against wind and rain, and if I go off to perform a natural function I am left with my legs frozen.'

Here ends Book I
Here begins the preface

In the preface to this little work I said I would follow three authorities only. But as the chief of these, Werinbert, died seven days ago and today (30 May) we, his bereaved sons and disciples, are going to pay solemn honour to his memory, here I will bring this book to an end, concerning the piety of Lord Charles and his care of the Church, which has been taken from the lips of this same cleric, Werinbert.

The next book, which deals with the wars of the most fierce Charles, is founded on the narrative of Werinbert's father, Adalbert. He followed his master Kerold in the Avar, Saxon and Slavic wars, and when I was quite a child, and he a very old man, I lived in his house and he used often to tell me the story of these events. I was most unwilling to listen and would often run away; but in the end by sheer force he made me hear.

THE SECOND BOOK OF THE DEEDS OF CHARLES

1. As I am going to found this narrative on the story told by a man of the world, who had little skill in letters, I think it will be well that I should first recall to memory something of our ancestors, following the testimony of writers. When Julian, whom God hated,[1] was slain in the Persian war by a blow from heaven, not only did the transmarine provinces fall away from the Roman Empire, but the neighbouring provinces of Pannonia, Noricum, Rhaetia and Germany also fell to the Franks or Gauls. Then, too, the kings of the Gauls or Franks began to decay in power because they had slain St Didier, bishop of Vienne, and had expelled those most holy visitors, Columban and Gall. Whereupon the race of the Avars, who had already often ravaged Francia and Aquitaine (that is to say, the two Gauls and the two Spains), now poured out with all their forces, devastated the whole land like a wide-sweeping conflagration, and then carried off all their spoils to a very safe hiding-place. What they were like, Adalbert, whom I have already mentioned, used to explain as follows: 'The land of the Avars', he would say, 'was surrounded by nine rings.' I could not think of any rings except our ordinary wicker fences for sheepfolds; and so I asked: 'What kind of wonder do you mean, master?' 'Well,' he replied, 'it was fortified by nine hedges.' I could not think of any hedges except those that protect our cornfields, so again I asked, and he answered: 'One ring was as wide, that is, it contained as much within it, as all the country between Tours and Konstanz. It was built out of logs of oak and ash and fir and was twenty feet wide and the same in height. All the space within was filled with very hard stones and binding clay; and

the surface of these ramparts was covered with great sods of earth. Within the limits of the ring small trees were planted of such a kind that, when lopped and bent down, as we often see done, they still threw out twigs and leaves. Then between these ramparts settlements and houses were so arranged that a man's voice could carry from one to the other. And opposite the buildings, at intervals in those unconquerable walls, were constructed doors of no great size; and through these doors the inhabitants from far and near would pour out on marauding expeditions. The second ring was like the first and was distant twenty Teutonic miles (or forty Italian) from the third ring; and so on to the ninth: though of course each successive ring was much smaller than the preceding one. But in all the circles the estates and houses were everywhere so arranged that the peal of trumpets would carry the news of any event from one to the other.'[2]

For two hundred years and more the Avars had swept the wealth of all of the western states within these fortifications, and as the Goths and Vandals were disturbing the repose of mortals they left the western world almost empty. But the most unconquerable Charles so subdued them in eight years that he allowed scarcely any traces of them to remain. He withdrew his hand from the Bulgars, because after the destruction of the Avars they did not seem likely to do any harm to the kingdom of the Franks. All the booty of the Avars, which he found in Pannonia, he divided most liberally among the bishoprics and the monasteries.

2. In the Saxon war, in which he was engaged in person for some considerable time, two private men (whose names I know, but modesty forbids me to give them) organized a storming party, and destroyed with great courage the walls of a very strong city and fortification. When the most just Charles saw this, with the consent of Kerold, who was the man's master, he made one of them commander of the country between the Rhine and the Italian Alps and the other he enriched with gifts of land.

3. At the same time there were the sons of two nobles whose duty it was to keep watch at the door of the king's tent. But

one night they lay as dead, soaked in liquor, while Charles, wakeful as usual, went the round of the camp, and came back to his tent without anyone having noticed him. When morning came he called to him all the great men of his kingdom, and asked them what punishment seemed fitting for those who betrayed the head of the Franks into the hands of the enemy. Then these nobles, quite ignorant of what had occurred, declared that such a man was worthy of death. But Charles merely upbraided them with the harshest words and let them go unharmed.

4. There were also with him two bastards, born in a brothel in Colmar. As they had fought most bravely, the emperor asked them whose children they were, and where they were born. When he was informed of the facts, he called them to his tent at midday and said: 'My good fellows, I want you to serve me, and no one else.' They exclaimed that they were there for that purpose and were ready to take even the lowest place in his service. 'Well then,' said Charles, 'you must serve in my chamber.' They concealed their indignation and said they would be glad to do so; but soon they seized the moment when the emperor had begun to sleep soundly, and then rushed out to the camp of the enemy and, in the fray that followed, wiped out the taint of servitude in their own blood and that of the enemy.[3]

5. Amid these sorts of activity the magnanimous emperor did not in any way cease from sending frequent messengers, carrying letters and presents, to the kings of the most distant regions; and they sent him in turn whatever honours their lands could bestow. From the scene of the Saxon war he sent messengers to the king of Constantinople; who asked them whether the kingdom of his son Charles was at peace or was being invaded by neighbouring peoples. Then the leader of the embassy made answer that peace reigned everywhere, except only that a certain race called the Saxons were disturbing the territories of the Franks by frequent raids. Whereupon the sluggish and unwarlike Greek king answered: 'Pooh! Why should my son take so much trouble about a petty enemy that possesses neither fame nor valour? I will give you the Saxon race and all that belong

to it.' When the envoy on his return gave this message to the most warlike Charles, he smiled and said: 'The king would have shown greater kindness to you if he had given you a linen leg-wrap for your long journey.'

6. I must not conceal the wise answer which the same envoy gave during his embassy to Greece. He came with his companions to one of the royal towns in the autumn; they were separated from each other, and the envoy of whom I speak was quartered on a certain bishop. This bishop spent all his time in fasting and prayer, and he mortified the envoy by giving him nothing to eat: but, with the first smile of spring, he presented the envoy to the king. The king asked him his opinion of the bishop. Then the envoy sighed from the very bottom of his heart and said: 'That bishop of yours reaches the highest point of holiness that can be attained without God.' The king was amazed and said: 'What! Can a man be holy without God?' Then said the envoy: 'It is written, "God is love," and in that he is entirely lacking.' Thereupon the king of Constantinople invited him to his banquet and placed him among his nobles. Now they had a law that no guest at the king's table, whether a native or a foreigner, should turn over any animal or part of an animal: he must eat only the upper part of whatever was placed before him. A river fish, covered with spice, was brought and placed on the dish before him. He knew nothing of the custom and turned the fish over, whereupon all the nobles rose up and cried: 'Master, you are dishonoured, as none of your ancestors ever was before you.' Then the king groaned and said to our envoy: 'I cannot resist them: you must be put to death at once; but ask me any other favour you like and I will grant it.' He thought awhile and then in the hearing of all pronounced these words: 'I pray you, lord emperor, that in accordance with your promise you will grant me one small petition.' And the king said: 'Ask what you will, and you shall have it: except only that I may not give you your life, for that is against the laws of the Greeks.' Then said the envoy: 'With my dying breath I ask one favour; let everyone who saw me turn that fish over be deprived of his eyes.' The king was amazed at the stipulation, and swore, by Christ, that he had seen nothing, but had only

trusted the word of others. Then the queen began to excuse herself: 'By the beneficent Mother of God, the Holy Mary, I noticed nothing.' Then the other nobles, in their desire to escape from the danger, swore, one by the keeper of the keys of heaven, and another by the apostle of the Gentiles, and all the rest by the virtue of the angels and the companies of the saints, that they were beyond the reach of the stipulation. And so the clever Frank beat the empty-headed sons of Hellas in their own land and came home safe and sound.

A few years later the unwearied Charles sent to Greece a certain bishop who was remarkable both for his mental and physical gifts, and with him the most noble duke Hugo. After a long delay they were at last brought into the presence of the king and then sent about to all manner of places. But at last they were sent back with great expenditure on their ship and their possessions.

Soon afterwards the Greek king sent his envoy to the most glorious Charles. It so happened that the bishop and the duke I have mentioned were just then with the emperor. When it was announced that the envoys were coming they advised the most wise Charles to have them led round through the Alps and pathless deserts, so that they should only come into the emperor's presence when their clothes had been worn and wasted and they were reduced to great want. This was done; and when at last they arrived, the bishop and his comrade bade the count of the stables take his seat on a high throne in the midst of his underlings, so that it was impossible to believe that he was anyone lower than the emperor. When the envoys saw him they fell upon the ground and wanted to worship him. But they were prevented by the servants and forced to go farther. Then they saw the count of the palace presiding over a gathering of the nobles and again they thought it was the emperor and flung themselves to earth. But those who were present drove them forward with blows and said: 'That is not the emperor.' Next they saw the master of the royal table surrounded by his noble band of servants; and again they fell to the ground think-ing that it was the emperor. Driven thence they found the chamberlains of the emperor and their chief in council together;

and then they did not doubt but that they were in the presence
of the first of living men. But this man too denied that he was
what they took him for; and yet he promised that he would use
his influence with the nobles of the palace, so that if possible
the envoys might come into the presence of the most august
emperor. Then there came servants from the imperial presence
to introduce them with full honours. Now Charles, the most
gracious of kings, was standing by an open window leaning
upon Bishop Heito, for that was the name of the bishop who
had been sent to Constantinople.[4] The emperor was clad in
gems and gold and glittered like the sun at its rising: and round
about him stood, as it were the chivalry of heaven, three young
men, his sons, who have since been made partners in the kingdom; his daughters and their mother, decorated with wisdom
and beauty as well as with pearls; leaders of the Church, unsurpassed in dignity and virtue; abbots distinguished for their high
birth and their sanctity; nobles, like Joshua when he appeared
in the camp of Gilgal; and an army like that which drove back
the Syrians and Assyrians out of Samaria.[5] If David had been
there he might well have sung: 'Kings of the earth and all
people; princes, and all judges of the earth; both young men,
and maidens; old men and children; let them praise the name
of the Lord.'[6] Then the envoys of the Greeks were astonished;
their spirit left them and their courage failed; speechless and
lifeless they fell upon the ground. But the most kindly emperor
raised them, and tried to cheer them with encouraging words.
At last life returned to them; but when they saw Heito, whom
they had once despised and rejected, now in so great honour,
again they grovelled on the ground in terror, until the King
swore to them by the King of heaven that he would do them
no harm. They took heart at this promise and began to act with
a little more confidence; and so home they went and never came
back again.

And here I must repeat that the most illustrious Charles had
men of the greatest cleverness in all offices.

7. When the morning Lauds had been celebrated before the
emperor on the octave of the Epiphany, the Greeks proceeded
privately to sing to God in their own language and he, hidden

nearby, was so pleased by the sweetness of the songs that he ordered his clerics to eat nothing until they had translated those antiphons into Latin and sung them to him. So it came to pass that all of them have been written in the same rhythm, and in one of them '*conteruit*' has been substituted for '*contrivit*'.[7]

These same Greek envoys brought with them every kind of organ, as well as other instruments of various kinds. All of these were secretly inspected by the workmen of the most wise Charles, and then exactly reproduced. The chief of these was that most remarkable of musicians' organs, in which the great chests were made of bronze, and the bellows of oxhide[8] blew through pipes of bronze, and the deep note was like the roaring of the thunder, and in sweetness it equalled the jangling of lyre or cymbal.[9] But I must not, here and now, speak of where it was set up, and how long it lasted, and how it perished at the same time as other losses.

8. About the same time, too, envoys of the Persians were sent to him. They did not know where Francia lay; but they thought it a great thing when they were able to reach the coast of Italy, because of the fame of Rome, over which they knew Charles ruled. They explained the reason of their journey to the bishops of Campania and Tuscany, of Emilia and Liguria, of Burgundy and Gaul, and to the abbots and counts of those regions; but they were either deceitfully handled by all of them or else actually driven away, so that a whole year had gone round before, weary and footsore with their long journey, they reached Aachen at last and saw Charles, the most renowned of kings by reason of his virtues. They arrived in the last week of Lent, and, on their arrival being made known to the emperor, he postponed seeing them until Easter Eve. Then, when that incomparable monarch was dressed with incomparable magnificence for the chief of festivals, he ordered the introduction of the envoys of that race that had once held the whole world in awe. But they were so terrified at the sight of the most magnificent Charles that one might think they had never seen a king or emperor before. He received them with great kindness, and granted them this privilege – that they might go wherever they had a mind to, as if they were his own children, and

examine everything and ask what questions and make what enquiries they chose. They jumped with joy at this favour, and valued the privilege of clinging close to Charles, of gazing upon him, of admiring him, more than all the wealth of the East. They went up into the solarium that runs round the nave of the cathedral and looked down upon the clergy and the army; then they returned to the emperor, and, by reason of the greatness of their joy, they could not refrain from laughing aloud; and they clapped their hands and said: 'We have seen only men of clay before: now we see gold.' Then they went to the nobles, one by one, and gazed with wonder upon arms and clothes that were strange to them; and then came back to the emperor, whom they regarded with still greater wonder. They passed that night and the next Sunday continuously in church; and, upon the most holy day itself, they were invited by the most munificent Charles to a splendid banquet, along with the nobles of Francia and Europe. There they were so struck with amazement at the strangeness of everything that they had hardly broken their fast.

> But when the Morn, leaving Tithonus' saffron bed,
> Illumined all the land with Phoebus' torch,[10]

then Charles, who could never endure idleness and sloth, went out to the woods to hunt the bison and the aurochs; and made preparations to take the Persian envoys with him. But when they saw the immense animals they were stricken with a mighty fear and turned and fled. But the undaunted hero Charles, riding on a high-spirited charger, drew near one of these animals and drawing his sword tried to cut through its neck. But he missed his aim, and the monstrous beast ripped the boot and leggings of the emperor; and, slightly wounding his calf with the tip of its horn, made him limp slightly: after that, furious at the failure of its stroke, it fled to the shelter of a valley, which was thickly covered with trees and stones. Nearly all his servants wanted to take off their own hose to give to Charles, but he forbade it saying: 'I mean to go in this fashion to Hildegard.' Then Isambard,[11] the son of Warin (the same Warin that persecuted your patron St Othmar), ran after the beast and, not daring to approach him more closely, threw his spear and pierced him to the heart between the shoulder and the windpipe, and brought the beast yet warm to the emperor. He seemed to pay no attention to the incident; but gave the carcass to his companions and went home. But then he called the queen and showed her how his leggings were torn, and said: 'What does the man deserve who freed me from the enemy that did this to me?' She made answer: 'He deserves the highest favour.' Then the emperor told the whole story and produced the enormous horns of the beast in witness of his truth: so that the empress sighed and wept and beat her breast. But when she heard that it was Isambard who had saved him from this terrible enemy, Isambard, who was hated and who had been deprived of all his offices, she threw herself at his feet and induced him to restore all that had been taken from him; and a reward was given to him in addition.

These same Persian envoys brought the emperor an elephant,[12] monkeys, balsam, nard, unguents of various kinds, spices, scents and many kinds of drugs, in such profusion that it seemed as if the East had been left bare so that the West might be filled. They soon came to be on very familiar terms with the emperor; and one day, when they were in an especially merry mood and a little heated with strong beer, they spoke in jest to the emperor, who was always armed with seriousness and sobriety, as follows: 'O emperor, your power is indeed great; but much less than the report of it which is spread through all the kingdoms of the East.' When he heard this he concealed his deep displeasure and asked jestingly of them: 'Why do you say that, my children? How did that idea get into your heads?' Then they went back to the beginning and told him everything that had happened to them in the lands beyond the sea; and they said: 'We Persians and the Medes, Armenians, Indians, Parthians, Elamites and all the inhabitants of the East fear you much more than our own ruler Harun.[13] And the Macedonians and all the Greeks (how shall we express it?) are beginning to fear your overwhelming greatness more than the waves of the Ionian Sea. And the inhabitants of all the islands through which we passed were as ready to obey you, and as much devoted to your service, as if they had been reared in your palace and loaded with great favours. But the nobles of your own kingdom, it seems to us, care very little about you except in your presence: for when we came as strangers to them, and begged them to show us some kindness for the love of you, to whom we desired to make our way, they gave no heed to us and sent us away empty-handed.' Then the emperor deposed all the counts and abbots through whose territories those envoys had come, from all the offices that they held; and fined the bishops by a huge sum of money. Then he ordered the envoys to be taken back to their own country with all care and honour.

9. There came to him also envoys from the king of the Africans, bringing a Marmarican[14] lion and a Numidian bear, with Spanish purple[15] and Tyrian murex, and other remarkable products of those regions. The most munificent Charles knew that the king and all the Libyans were oppressed by constant poverty; and so, not only on this occasion but all through his life, he made them presents of the wealth of Europe, corn and wine and oil, and gave them liberal support; and thus he kept them constantly loyal and obedient to himself, and received from them a considerable tribute.

Soon after this the unwearied emperor sent to the emperor of the Persians horses and mules from Spain and Frisian robes, white, grey, crimson and blue, which in Persia, he was told, were rarely seen and highly prized. Dogs too he sent him of remarkable swiftness and fierceness, such as the king of Persia had desired, for hunting and driving away lions and tigers. The king of Persia cast a careless eye over the other presents, but asked the envoys what wild beasts or animals these dogs were accustomed to subdue. He was told that they would pull down quickly anything they were set onto. 'Well,' he said, 'experience will test that.' Next day the shepherds were heard crying loudly as they fled from a lion. When the noise came to the palace of the king, he said to the envoys: 'Now, my Frankish friends, mount your horses and follow me.' Then they followed eagerly after the king as though they had never known toil or weariness.

When they came in sight of the lion, though he was still at a distance, the satrap of the satraps said to them: 'Now set your dogs onto the lion.' They obeyed and eagerly galloped forward; the German dogs caught the Persian lion, and the envoys slew him with swords of northern metal, which had already been tempered in blood.

At this sight Haroun, the strongest heir to that name,[16] understood the superior might of Charles from these very small matters, and broke out in his praise with these words: 'Now I know that what I heard of my brother Charles is true: how that by the frequent practice of hunting, and by the unwearied training of his body and mind, he has acquired the habit of subduing all that is beneath the heavens. How can I make worthy recompense for the honours he has bestowed upon me? If I give him the land which was promised to Abraham and shown to Joshua, it is so far away that he could not defend it from the barbarians: or if, like the magnanimous king he is, he tried to defend it I fear that the provinces which lie upon the frontiers of the Frankish kingdom would leave his empire. But in this way I will try to show my gratitude for his generosity. I will give that land into his power; and I will rule over it as his representative. Whenever he likes or whenever there is a good opportunity, he shall send me envoys; and he will find me a faithful manager of the revenue of that province.'

Thus was brought to pass what the poet spoke of as an impossibility: 'Either the Parthian shall drink the Arar or Germany the Tigris';[17] for through the energy of the most vigorous Charles it was found not merely possible but quite easy for his envoys to go and return; and the messengers of Haroun, whether young or old, passed easily from Parthia into Germany and returned from Germany to Parthia (and the poet's words are true, whatever interpretation the grammarians put on 'the River Arar', whether they think it a tributary of the Rhône or the Rhine; for they have fallen into confusion on this point through their ignorance of the locality). I could call on the whole of Germany to bear witness to my words; for in the time of your glorious father Louis the land was compelled to pay a penny for every acre of land held under the law towards the redemption of Christians living in the Holy Land; and they made their wretched appeal in the name of the dominion anciently held over that land by your great-grandfather Charles and your grandfather Louis.

10. Now as the occasion has arisen to make honourable mention of your father,[18] who can never be praised enough, I should like to recall some prophetic words which the most wise Charles is known to have uttered about him. When he was six years old and had been most carefully reared in the house of his father, he was thought (and justly) to be wiser than men sixty years of age. Then his most tender father, hardly thinking it possible that he could bring him to see his grandfather, nevertheless took him from his mother, who had reared him most luxuriously, and began to instruct him how to conduct himself with propriety and modesty in the presence of the emperor; and how if he were asked a question he was to answer him and show in all things deference to his father. Thereafter he took him to the palace; and, on the first or second day, the emperor noted him with interest standing among the rest of the courtiers. 'Whose is that little fellow?' he said to his son; and he had for answer: 'He is mine, sire; and yours, if you deign to have him.' So he said: 'Give him to me'; and, when that was done, he took the little fellow and kissed him and sent him back to the place where he had formerly stood. But now he knew his own rank; and thought it shame to stand lower than anyone who was lower in rank than the emperor; so with perfect composure of mind and body he took his place on terms of equality with his father. The most prophetic Charles noticed this; and, calling his son Louis, told him to find out the name of the boy; and why he acted in this way; and what it was that made him bold enough to claim equality with his father. The answer Louis got was founded on good reason: 'When I was your vassal,' he said, 'I stood behind you and among soldiers of my own rank, as I was bound to do: but now I am your ally and comrade in arms, and so I rightly claim equality with you.' When Louis reported this to the emperor, the latter gave utterance to words something like these: 'If that little fellow lives he will be something great.' (I have borrowed these words from the Life of

St Ambrose,[19] because the actual words that Charles used cannot be translated directly into Latin. And it seems fair to apply the prophecy which was made of St Ambrose to Louis; for Louis closely resembled the saint, except in such points as are necessary to an earthly commonwealth, as for instance marriage and the use of arms; and in the power of his kingdom and his zeal for religion, Louis was, if I may say so, superior to St Ambrose.) He was a Catholic in faith, devoted to the worship of God, and the unwearied ally, protector and defender of the servants of Christ. Here is an instance of this. When our faithful abbot Hartmut[20] – who is now your hermit – reported to him that the small endowment of St Gall, which was due not to royal endowments but to the petty offerings of private people, was not defended by any special charter such as other monasteries have, nor even by the laws that are common to all peoples, and so was unable to procure any defender or advocate, King Louis himself took a stand against all our opponents, and was not ashamed to proclaim himself the champion of our weakness in the presence of all his nobles.[21] At the same time, too, he wrote a letter to your genius directing that we should have licence to make petition, after taking a special vote, for whatever we would need through your authority. But alas, what a stupid creature I am! I have probably been drawn aside by my personal gratitude for the special kindness he showed us, away from his general and indescribable goodness and greatness and nobleness.

11. Now Louis, king and emperor of all Germany, of the provinces of Rhaetia and of ancient Francia, of Saxony too and of Thuringia, of the provinces of Pannonia and of all northern nations, was of fine stature and handsome appearance; his eyes sparkled like the stars, his voice was clear and manly. His wisdom was quite out of the common, and he added to it by constantly applying his singularly acute intellect to the study of the Scriptures. He showed wonderful quickness, too, in anticipating or overcoming the plots of his enemies, in bringing to an end the quarrels of his subjects and in procuring every kind of advantage for those who were loyal to him. Even more than

his ancestors he came to be a terror to all the heathen peoples
who stood round about his kingdom. And he deserved his good
fortune; for he never broke his word in judgement; nor defiled
his hands by shedding Christian blood, except once only, and
then upon the most absolute necessity.[22] But I dare not tell that
story until I see a little Louis or a Charles standing by your side.
After that one slaughter, nothing could induce him to condemn
anyone to death. But the measure of compulsion which he used
against those who were accused of disloyalty or plots was
merely this: he deprived them of office, and no new circum-
stance and no length of time could then soften his heart so as
to restore them to the former rank. He surpassed all men in his
zealous devotion to prayer, religious fasting and the care for
the worship of God; and like St Martin, whatever he was doing,
he prayed to God as though he were face to face with Him.[23]
On certain days he abstained from flesh and all fine foods. At
the time of litanies he used to follow the cross barefoot from
his palace as far as the cathedral;[24] or if he were at Regensburg
as far as the church of St Emmeram. In other places he followed
the customs of those he was with.[25] He built new oratories of
wonderful workmanship at Frankfurt and Regensburg.[26] In the
latter place, as stones were wanting to complete the immense
fabric, he ordered the walls of the city to be pulled down; and
in certain holes in the wall they found bones of men long dead,
wrapped in so much gold that not only did it serve to decorate
the cathedral but he was also able to furnish certain books that
were written on the subject with bindings of the same material
nearly a finger thick. No clerk could stay with him, or even
come into his presence, unless he was skilled in reading and
chanting. He despised monks who broke their vows, and loved
those who kept them. He was so full of sweet-tempered mirth,
that if anyone came to him who was sad, merely to see him and
exchange a few words with him, he sent the visitor away with
raised spirits. If anything evil or foolish was done in his presence, or if it happened that he were told of it, a single glance of
his eyes was enough to check everything, so that what is written
of the eternal judge who sees the hearts of men: 'A king that

sitteth in the throne of judgement scattereth away all evil with His eyes',[27] might be fairly said to have begun in him, beyond what is usually granted to mortals.

All this I have written by way of digression, hoping that, if life lasts and heaven is propitious, I may in time to come to write much more concerning him.

12. But I must return to my subject. While Charles was detained for a little at Aachen by the arrival of many visitors and the hostility of the unconquered Saxons and the robbery and piracy of the Northmen and Moors, and while the war against the Avars was being conducted by his son Pippin, the barbarous nations coming from the north attacked Noricum and Eastern Francia and ravaged a great part of it. When he heard of this he humbled them himself; and he gave orders that all the boys and children of the invaders should be 'measured with the sword';[28] and if anyone exceeded that measurement he should be shortened by a head.

This incident led to another, much greater and more important. For, when your imperial majesty's most holy grandfather departed this life, certain giants (like those who, Scripture tells us, were begotten by the sons of Seth from the daughters of Cain), blown up with the spirit of pride, and doubtless like to those who said: 'What portion have we in David and what inheritance in the son of Jesse?'[29] – these mighty men, I say, despised the most worthy children of Charles, and each tried to seize for himself the command in the kingdom and themselves to wear the crown. Then some of the middling sort were moved by the inspiration of God to declare that, as the renowned emperor Charles had once measured the enemies of the Christians with the sword, so, as long as any of his progeny could be found of the length of a sword, he must rule over the Franks and over all Germany too: thereupon that devilish group of conspirators was as it were struck with a thunderbolt, and scattered in all directions.

But, after conquering the external foe, Charles was oppressed by his own people in a remarkable but vain plot. For on his return from the Slavs to Regensburg he was nearly captured and put to death by his son, whom a concubine had borne to him and who had been called by his mother by the ill-omened name of the most glorious Pippin. The plot was found out in the following way. This son of Charles had been plotting the death of the emperor with a gathering of nobles, in the church of St Peter; and when their debate was over, afraid of what is harmless, he ordered a search to be made to see whether anyone was hidden in the corners or under the altars. And behold, they found, as they feared, a cleric hidden under an altar. They seized him and made him swear that he would not reveal their conspiracy. To save his life, he dared not refuse to take the oath which they dictated: but, when they were gone, he held his wicked oath of small account and at once hurried to the palace. With the greatest difficulty he passed through the seven bolted gates, and coming at length to the emperor's chamber knocked upon the door. The most vigilant Charles fell into great astonishment as to who it was that dared to disturb him at that time of night. However, he ordered the women (who followed in his train to wait upon the queen and her daughters) to go out and see who was at the door and what he wanted. When they went out and found the wretched creature, they bolted the door in his face and then, bursting with laughter and stuffing their dresses into their mouths, they tried to hide themselves in the corners of the apartments. But the wisest of emperors, whose notice nothing under heaven could escape, questioned the women closely about what the matter was and who was knocking at the door. When he was told that it was a shaven, silly, half-mad knave, dressed only in shirt and drawers, who demanded an audience without delay, Charles ordered him to be admitted. Then he fell at the emperor's feet and revealed all that had happened. So all the conspirators, entirely unsuspicious of danger, were seized before the third hour of the day and most deservedly condemned to exile or some other form of punishment. Pippin himself, a dwarf and a hunchback, was cruelly scourged, tonsured and sent for some time as a punishment to the monastery of St Gall; the poorest, it was judged, and the most austere in all the emperor's broad dominions.

A short time afterwards some of the Frankish nobles sought to do violence to their king. Charles was well aware of their intentions, and yet did not wish to destroy them; because if only they were loyal they might be a great protection to all Christian men. So he sent messengers to this Pippin, and asked him what he ought to do with them. They found him in the monastery garden, in the company of the older brothers, for the younger ones were detained by more serious work. He was digging up nettles and other weeds with a three-pronged fork, so that the useful herbs might grow more vigorously. When they had explained to him the reason for their coming he sighed deeply, from the very bottom of his heart, for all deformed people tend to be more irritable than those who are properly proportioned, and said in reply: 'If Charles thought my advice worth having he would not have treated me so harshly. I give him no advice. Go, tell him what you found me doing.' They were afraid to go back to the dread emperor without a definite answer, and again and again asked him what message they should convey to their lord. Then at last he said in anger: 'I will send him no message except – what I am doing! I am digging up the useless weeds in order that the valuable vegetables may be able to develop more freely.'

So they went away sorrowfully, thinking that they were bringing back a foolish answer. When the emperor asked them on their arrival what answer they were bringing, they answered that after all their labour and long journeying they could get no definite information at all. Then that most wise king asked them carefully where they had found Pippin, and what he was doing, and what answer he had given them; and they said: 'We found him sitting on a rustic three-legged stool turning over the vegetable garden with a three-pronged fork. When we told him the cause of our journey we could extract no other reply than is, even by the greatest entreaties: "I give no message except – what I am doing! I am digging up the useless growths in order that the useful vegetables may be able to develop more freely."'
When he heard this, the emperor, not lacking in cunning and mighty in wisdom, rubbed his ears and blew out his nostrils and said: 'My good vassals, you have brought back a very reasonable answer.' So, while the messengers feared they might be in peril of their lives, Charles was able to divine the real

meaning of the words. He took all those plotters away from the land of the living; and so gave to his loyal subjects room to grow and spread, which had previously been occupied by those unprofitable servants. One of his enemies, who had chosen as part of the spoil of the empire the highest hill in Francia and all that could be seen from it, was, by Charles's orders, hanged upon a high gallows on that very hill. But he bade his bastard son Pippin choose the manner of life that most pleased him. Upon this permission being given him, he chose a post in a monastery that was then most noble but is now destroyed.[30] (Who is there that does not know the manner of its destruction! But I will not tell the story of its fall until I see your little Bernard with a sword girt upon his thigh.)

The magnanimous Charles was often angry because he was urged to go out and fight against foreign nations, when one of his nobles might have accomplished the task. I can prove this from the action of one of my own neighbours. There was a man of Thurgau, named Eishere, who as his name implies was 'a great part of a terrible army' and so tall that you might have thought him sprung from the race of Anak,[31] if they had not lived so long ago and so far away. Whenever he came to the River Thur and found it swollen and foaming with the torrents from the mountains, and could not force his huge warhorse to enter the stream (though stream I must not call it, but barely melted ice), then he would seize the reins and force his warhorse to swim through behind him, saying: 'Nay, by St Gall, you must come, whether you like it or not!'

Well, this man followed the emperor and mowed down the Bohemians and the Wiltzi and Avars as a man might mow down hay; and spitted them on his spear like little birds. When he came home the sluggards asked him how he had got on in the country of the Winides; and he, contemptuous of some and angry with others, replied: 'Why should I have been bothered with those tadpoles? I used sometimes to spit seven or eight or nine of them on my spear and carry them about with me squealing I know not what. My lord king and I ought never to have been asked to weary ourselves in fighting against worms like those.'

13. Now about the same time the emperor was putting the finishing touch to the war with the Avars, and had received the surrender of the races that I have just mentioned, the Northmen left their homes and disquieted greatly the Gauls and the Franks. Then the unconquered Charles returned and tried to attack them by land in their own homes, by a march through difficult and unknown country. But whether it was that the providence of God prevented it in order that, as the Scripture says, He might prove Israel,[32] or whether it was that our sins stood in the way, all his efforts came to nothing. One night, to the serious discomfort of the whole army, it was calculated that fifty yoke of oxen belonging to one abbey had died of a sudden disease. Charlemagne, who was the wisest of men, decided to abandon his plan lest he disobey the Scripture by 'trying to move against the cunning of the stream'.[33] Afterwards, when Charles was making a prolonged journey through his vast empire, Godfrid, king of the Northmen, encouraged by his absence, invaded the territory of the king of the Franks and chose the district of the Moselle for his home.[34] But Godfrid's own son (whose mother he had just abandoned and he had taken to himself a new wife) caught him, while he was pulling his hawk off a heron, and cut him through the middle with his sword. Then, as happened of old when Holofernes[35] was slain, no one dared trust any longer in his courage or his arms; but all sought safety in flight. And thus the Franks were freed without any effort of their own, so that they might not after the fashion of ungrateful Israel boast to God. Then Charles, the unconquered and the invincible, glorified God for His judgement; but complained bitterly that any of the Northmen had escaped because of his absence. 'Ah, woe is me,' he said, 'that I was not thought worthy to see my Christian hands dabbling in the blood of those dog-headed fiends!'

14. It happened too that on his wanderings Charles once came unexpectedly to a certain maritime city of Narbonensis. When he was dining quietly it happened that some Norman scouts made a piratical raid on the harbour. When the ships came in sight some thought them Jews, some African or British merchants, but the most wise Charles, by the build of the ships

and their speed, knew them to be not merchants but enemies, and said to his companions: 'These ships are not filled with merchandise, but crowded with our fiercest enemies.' When they heard this, in eager rivalry, they hurried in haste to the ships. But all was in vain, for when the Northmen heard that Charles, the Hammer as they used to call him, was there, fearing lest their fleet should be beaten back or even smashed in pieces, they withdrew themselves, by a marvellously rapid flight, not only from the swords but even from the eyes of those who followed them. The most religious, just and devout Charles had risen from the table and was standing at an eastern window. For a long time he shed tears beyond price, and none dared speak a word to him; but at last he explained his actions and his tears to his nobles in these words: 'Do you know why I weep so bitterly, my true servants? I have no fear of those worthless jokers doing any harm to me; but I am sad at heart to think that even during my lifetime they have dared to touch this shore; and I am torn by a great sorrow because I foresee what evil things they will do to my descendants and their subjects.'

May the protection of Christ our Lord prevent this from happening; and may your sword, tempered already in the blood of the Nordostrani, resist it! The sword of your brother Carloman will help,[36] which now lies idle and rusted, not through cowardice, but for want of funds, and because of the narrowness of the lands of your most faithful servant Arnulf.[37] If your might wills it, if your might orders it, it will easily be made bright and sharp again. This one small bough and the little shoot of Bernard form the only branch that is left of the once prolific root of Louis, to flourish under the wonderful growth of your protection. Let me insert here therefore in the history of your namesake Charles an incident in the life of your great-great-grandfather Pippin: which perhaps some future little Charles or Louis may imitate.

15. When the Lombards and other enemies were attacking the Romans, they sent ambassadors to this same Pippin, and asked him for the love of St Peter to condescend to come with all speed to their help. As soon as he had conquered his enemies

he came as victor to Rome to pray and this was the song of praise with which the citizens received him. 'The fellow-citizens of the apostles and the servants of God have come today bringing peace, and making their native land glorious, to give peace to the heathen and to set free the people of the Lord.' (Many people, ignorant of the meaning and origin of this song, have been accustomed to sing it on the birthdays of the apostles.[38]) Pippin feared the envy of the people of Rome (or, more truly, of Constantinople) and soon returned to Francia.

When he found out that the nobles of his army were accustomed in secret to speak contemptuously of him, he ordered one day a bull, terrible in size, to be brought out, and then a most savage lion to be let loose upon him. The lion rushed with tremendous fury on the bull, seized him by the neck and cast him to the ground. Then the king said to those who stood round him: 'Now, drag the lion off the bull, or kill the one on the top of the other.' They looked at one another, with a chill in their hearts, and could hardly utter these words amid their gasps: 'Lord, there is no man under heaven, who dare attempt it.' Then Pippin rose confidently from his throne, drew his sword, and at one blow cut through the neck of the lion and severed the head of the bull from his shoulders. Then he put his sword back into its sheath and sat down on his throne and said: 'Well, do you think I am fit to be your lord? Have you not heard what little David did to the giant Goliath, or what tiny Alexander did to his nobles?' They fell to the ground, as though a thunderbolt had struck them, and cried: 'Who but a madman would deny your right to rule over all mankind?'

Not only did he perform such feats against beasts and men; but he also fought an incredible contest against evil spirits. The hot baths at Aachen had not yet been built; but hot and healing waters bubbled forth from the ground. He ordered his chamberlain to see that the water was clean and that no unknown person had been allowed to enter. This was done; and the king took his sword and, dressed only in a linen gown and slippers, hurried off to the bath; when lo! the old enemy met him, and attacked him as though he would slay him. But the king protected himself with the sign of the cross, drew his sword;

and, noticing a shape in human form, struck his invincible
sword through it into the ground, so far that he could only
drag it out again after a long struggle. But the shape was of
such thickness that it defiled all those waters with blood and
gore and revolting slime. But even this did not trouble the
unconquerable Pippin. He said to his chamberlain: 'Do not
mind this little affair. Let the defiled water run for a while; and
then, when it flows clear again, I will take my bath at once.'

16. I had intended, most noble emperor, to weave my short
little narrative only round your great-grandfather Charles, all
of whose deeds you know well. But since the occasion arose
which made it necessary to mention your most glorious father
Louis, called the illustrious, and your most religious grandfather Louis, called the Pious, and your most warlike great-
great-grandfather Pippin the younger, I thought it would be
wrong to pass over their deeds in silence, for the sloth of modern
writers has left them almost untold. There is no need to speak of
the elder Pippin, for the most learned Bede in his *Ecclesiastical
History* has devoted nearly a whole book to him.[39] But now
that I have recounted all these things by way of digression I must
swim, swan-like, back to your illustrious namesake Charles. But
if I do not curtail somewhat his feats in war, I shall never come
to consider his daily habits of life. Now I will give with all
possible brevity the incidents that occur to me

17. When after the death of the ever-victorious Pippin the
Lombards were again attacking Rome, the unconquered
Charles, though he was fully occupied to the north of the Alps,
marched swiftly into Italy. He received the Lombards into his
service after they had been humbled in a war that was almost
bloodless, or (one might say), after they had surrendered of
their own free will; and to prevent them from ever again revolting from the Frankish kingdom, or doing any injury to the
territories of St Peter, he married the daughter of Desiderius,
king of the Lombards.[40] But shortly afterwards, because she
was an invalid and unable to bear a child, she was, by the
counsel of the holiest of the clergy, put aside, as if she were
dead: whereupon her father in wrath bound his subjects to him
by oath, and, shutting himself up within the walls of Pavia, he

prepared to give battle to the invincible Charles, who, when he had received certain news of the revolt, hurried to Italy with all speed.

Now it happened that some years before, one of the chief nobles, called Otker, had incurred the wrath of the most dread emperor, and had fled for refuge to Desiderius. When they heard that the fearsome Charles was approaching, these two went up into a very high tower, from which they could see anyone approaching at a very great distance. When therefore the baggage-wagons appeared, which moved more swiftly than those used by Darius or Julius, Desiderius said to Otker: 'Is Charles in that vast army?' And Otker answered: 'Not yet.' Then when he saw the vast force of the nations gathered together from all parts of his empire, he said with confidence to Otker: 'Surely Charles moves proudly among those forces.' But Otker answered: 'Not yet, not yet.' Then Desiderius fell into great alarm and said: 'What shall we do if a yet greater force comes with him?' And Otker said, 'You will see what he is like when he comes. What will happen to us I cannot say.' And, behold, while they were thus talking there came in sight Charles's retinue, who never rested from their labours; and Desiderius saw them and cried in amazement: 'There is Charles.' And Otker answered: 'Not yet, not yet.' Then they saw the bishops and the abbots and the clerics of his chapel with their attendants. When he saw them he hated the light and longed for death, and sobbed and stammered: 'Let us go down to hide ourselves in the earth from the face of the fury of an enemy so terrible.' And Otker answered, trembling, for once, in happier days, he had had thorough and constant knowledge of the policy and preparations of the unconquerable Charles: 'When you see the fields bristling with iron corn; and the Po and the Ticino pouring against the walls of the city like the waves of the sea, gleaming black with glint of iron, then know that Charles is at hand.' Hardly were these words finished when there came from the west a mighty wind and with it the north wind began to blow like a black cloud, which turned the bright day to horrid gloom. But as the emperor drew nearer the gleam of his weapons turned the darkness into day, a day darker than any night to that beleaguered garrison. Then could be seen the iron Charles, helmeted with an iron helmet, his hands clad in iron gauntlets, his iron breast and Platonic shoulders protected with an iron breastplate: an iron spear was raised on high in his left hand; his right always rested on his unconquered sword. The thighs, which with most men are uncovered so that they may the more easily ride on horseback, were in his case clad with plates of iron: I need make no special mention of his greaves, for the greaves of all the army were of iron. His shield was all of iron: his warhorse was iron-coloured and iron-hearted. All who went before him, all who marched by his side, all who followed after him and the whole equipment of the army imitated him as closely as possible. The fields and open places were filled with iron; the rays of the sun were thrown back by the gleam of iron; a people harder than iron paid universal honour to the hardness of iron. The horror of the dungeon seemed less than the bright gleam of iron. 'Oh, the iron! Woe for the iron!' was the confused cry that rose from the citizens. The strong walls shook at the sight of the iron; the resolution of young and old fell before the iron. Now when the truthful Otker saw in one swift glance all this which I, a tooth-less man with stammering tongue, have been clumsily explain-ing with rambling words, he said to Desiderius: 'There is the Charles that you so much desired to see': and when he had said this he fell to the ground half-dead.

But as the inhabitants of the city, either through madness or because they had some hope of resistance, refused to let Charles enter on that day, the most ingenious emperor said to his men: 'Let us build today something memorable, so that we may not be charged with passing the day in idleness. Let us make haste to build for ourselves a little house of prayer, where we may give due attention to the service of God, if they do not soon throw open the city to us.' No sooner had he said it than his men flew off in every direction, collected lime and stones, wood and paint, and brought them to the skilled workmen who always accompanied him. And between the fourth hour of the day and the twelfth they built, with the help of the young nobles and the soldiers, such a basilica, so provided with walls and roofs, with panelled ceilings and frescoes, that none who saw it could believe that it had taken less than a year to build. But, how on the next day some of the citizens wanted to throw open the gate; and some wanted to fight against him, even without hope of victory, or rather to fortify themselves against him; and how easily he conquered, took and occupied the city, without the shedding of blood, and merely by the exercise of skill; all this I must leave to others to tell, who follow your highness not for love, but in the hope of gain.[41]

Then the most religious Charles marched on and came to the city of Friuli, which the pedants call Forum Julii.[42] Now it happened just at this time that the bishop of that city (or, to use a modern word, the patriarch) was drawing near to the end of his life. Charles made haste to visit him, in order that he might designate his successor by name. But the bishop, with remarkable piety, sighed from the bottom of his heart and said: 'Sire, I have held this bishopric for a long time without any use or profit; and now I leave it to the judgement of God and your direction. For I do not wish, at the point of death, to add anything to the mountain of sins I have heaped together during my life, for which I shall have to make answer to the inevitable and incorruptible judge.' The most wise Charles was so pleased with these words, that he rightly thought him the equal in virtue of the ancient fathers.

After Charles, the most energetic of all the energetic Franks, had stayed in that country for a short time, while he was appointing a worthy successor to the deceased bishop, one festal day after the celebration of Mass he said to his retinue: 'We must not let leisure lead us into slothful habits: let us go hunting and kill something; and let us all go in the very clothes that we are wearing at this moment.' Now the day was cold and rainy and Charles was wearing a sheepskin, not much more costly than the cloak which St Martin wore when with bare arms he offered to God a sacrifice that received divine approval.[43] But the others – for it was a holiday and they had just come from Pavia, whither the Venetians had carried all the wealth of the East from their territories beyond the sea[44] – the other, I say, strutted in robes made of pheasant-skins surrounded with silk; or of the necks, backs and tails of peacocks in their first plumage. Some were decorated with Tyrian purple and lemon-coloured ribbons; some were wrapped round with otter-skins and some in ermine robes. They scoured the thickets; they were torn by branches of trees, thorns and briars; they were drenched with rain; they were defiled with the blood of wild beasts and the filth of the skins; and in this plight they returned home. Then the most cunning Charles said: 'No one of us must take off his dress of skins before he goes to bed; they will dry better upon our bodies.' Then everyone, more anxious about his body than his dress, sought out fires and tried to warm himself. Then they returned and remained in attendance upon Charles far into the night before they were dismissed to their apartments. Then when they began to draw off their delicate dresses of skins and their slender belts, the creased and shrunken garments could be heard even from a distance cracking, like sticks broken when they are dry: and the courtiers sighed and groaned and lamented that they had lost so much money on a single day. They had received, however, a command from the emperor to appear before him next day in the same skin-garments. When they came it was no longer the splendid show of yesterday; for they looked dirty and squalid in their discoloured and torn clothes. Then Charles, full of activity, said to his chamberlain: 'Give my sheepskin a rub and bring it to me.' It came quite white and perfectly sound and Charles took it and showed it to all those who were there and spoke as follows: 'Most foolish of mortal men! Which of these dresses is the most valuable and the most useful, this one of mine which was bought for a piece of silver, or those of yours which you bought for pounds, nay for many talents?' Their eyes sank to the ground for they could not bear his most terrible censure.[45]

Your most religious father imitated this example not once but throughout his life, for he never allowed anyone who seemed to him worthy of his notice or his teaching to wear anything when on campaign against the enemy except military equipment and woollen garments and linen. If any of his servants, ignorant of this rule, happened to meet him with silk or gold or silver upon his person, he would receive a reprimand of the following kind and would depart a better and a wiser man: 'Here's a blaze of gold and silver and scarlet! Why, you wretched fellow, can't you be satisfied with perishing yourself in battle if Fate so decides? Must you also give your wealth into the hands of the enemy; which might have gone to ransom your soul, but now will decorate the idols of the heathen?'

But now, though you know it better than I do, I will tell again how, from early youth up to his seventieth year, the unconquered Louis delighted in iron; and what an exhibition of his fondness for iron he made in the presence of the legates of the Northmen!

18. When the kings of the Northmen each sent him gold and silver as a sign of their loyalty, and their own swords as a mark of their perpetual subjection and surrender, the king gave orders that the precious metals should be thrown on the floor, and should be looked upon by all with contempt, and be trampled upon by all as though they were dirt. But, as he sat upon his lofty throne, he ordered the swords to be brought to him that he might test them. Then the ambassadors, anxious to avoid the possibility of any suspicion of an evil design, took the swords by the point (as servants hand knives to their masters) and thus gave them to the emperor at their own risk. He took one by the hilt and tried to bend the tip of the blade right back to the base; but the blade snapped between his hands, which were stronger than the iron itself. Then one of the envoys drew his own sword from its sheath and offered it, like a servant, to the emperor's service, saying: 'I think you will find this sword as flexible and as strong as your all-conquering right hand could desire.' Then the emperor took the sword (a true emperor he!) As the prophet Isaiah says in his prophecy, 'Look to the rock whence ye were hewn';[46] for he alone out of all the vast population of Germany, by the singular favour of God, rose to the level of the strength and courage of an earlier generation – the emperor, I say, bent it like a vine-twig from the extreme tip back to the hilt, and then let it gradually straighten itself again. Then the envoys gazed upon one another and said in amazement: 'Would that our kings held gold and silver so cheap and iron so precious.'[47]

19. As I have mentioned the Northmen I will show by an incident drawn from the reign of your grandfather in what slight estimation they hold faith and baptism. Just as after the death of the most warlike king David, the neighbouring peoples, whom his strong hand had subdued, for a long time paid their tribute to his peaceful son Solomon: even so the terrible race of the Northmen still loyally paid to Louis the tribute which through terror they had paid to his father, the most august emperor Charles. Once the most religious emperor Louis took pity on their envoys, and asked them if they would be willing to receive the Christian religion; and, when they answered that they were ready to obey him always and everywhere and in everything, he ordered them to be baptized in the name of Him, of whom the most learned Augustine says: 'If there were no Trinity, the Truth would never have said: "Go and teach all peoples, baptizing them in the name of the Father, Son and Holy Spirit." '[48] The nobles of the palace adopted them almost as children, and each received from the emperor's chamber a white robe and from their sponsors a full set of Frankish garments, of costly robes and arms and other adornments. This was often done and from year to year they came in increasing numbers, not for the sake of Christ but for earthly advantages. They made haste to come – not as envoys any longer but as most loyal vassals – on Easter Eve to put themselves at the disposal of the emperor; and it happened that on a certain occasion as many as fifty came. The emperor asked them whether they wished to be baptized, and when they had confessed he bade them forthwith be sprinkled with holy water. As linen garments were not ready in sufficient numbers he ordered shirts to be cut up and sewn together into the fashion of tunics. One of these was immediately put on one of the older men; and when he had looked all over it for a minute, he conceived fierce anger in his mind, and said to the emperor: 'I have gone through this washing business here twenty times already, and I have been dressed in excellent clothes of perfect whiteness; but a sack like this is more fit for swineherds than for soldiers. If I were not afraid of my nakedness, for you have taken away my own clothes and have given

me no new ones, I would soon leave your wrap and your Christ as well.'

How little do the enemies of Christ value the words of the apostle of Christ where he says: 'For as many of you as have been baptized in Christ, have put on Christ';[49] and again: 'So many of us as were baptized into Christ Jesus were baptized into His death';[50] or that passage which is aimed especially at those who despise the faith and violate the sacraments: 'Crucifying the Son of God afresh and putting Him to an open shame!'[51] Oh! would that this were the case only with the heathen; and not also among those who are called by the name of Christ!

20. Now I must tell a story about the goodness of the first Louis, and then I shall come back to Charles. That most peaceable emperor Louis, being free from all incursions of the enemy, gave all his care to works of religion, as, for instance, to prayer, to works of charity, to the hearing and just determinations of law cases. His talents and his experience had made him very skilful in this kind of business; and when one day someone came to him who was considered a very Achitophel[52] by all, and tried to deceive him, he gave him this answer following, with a friendly face and a kindly voice, though with some little agitation of mind: 'Most wise Anselm,'[53] he said, 'if I may be allowed to say so, I would venture to observe that you are deviating from the path of rectitude.' From that day the reputation of that legal luminary sank to nothing in the eyes of all the world.

21. The most compassionate Louis was so intent on works of charity that he liked not merely to have them done in his sight, but even to do them with his own hand. Even when he was away he made special arrangements for the trial of lawsuits in which the poor were concerned. He chose one of their own number, a man very weak in every limb, but apparently more courageous than the rest, and gave orders that he should decide offences committed by them; and should see to the restoration of stolen property, the requital of injuries and wounds, and in cases of greater crimes to the cutting off of limbs, decapitation and the exposure of the bodies on the gallows. This man estab-

lished dukes, tribunes, centurions and their representatives, and performed his task with energy.

Moreover the most merciful emperor, worshipping Christ in the persons of all the poor, was never weary of giving them food and clothing;[54] and he did so especially on the day when Christ, having put off His mortal body, was preparing to take to Himself an incorruptible one. On that day it was his practice to make presents to each and every one of those who served in the palace or did duty in the royal court. He would order belts, leg-coverings and precious garments to be brought from all parts of his vast empire and given to some of his nobles; the lower orders would get Frisian cloaks of various colours; his grooms, cooks and kitchen-attendants got clothes of linen and wool and knives according to their needs. Then, when according to the Acts of the Apostles there was none among them that lacked,[55] there was a universal feeling of gratitude. The ragged poor, now decently clad, raised their voices to heaven with the cry of 'Kyrie Eleison to the blessed Louis' through all the wide courts and the smaller openings of Aachen (which the Latins usually call porches); and all the soldiers who could embraced the feet of the emperor; and those who could not get to him worshipped him afar off as he made his way to church. On one of these occasions one of the court jesters said facetiously: 'O happy Louis, who on one day have been able to clothe so many people. By Christ, I think that no one in Europe has clothed more than you this day, except Atto.' When the emperor asked him how it was possible that Atto should have clothed more, the jester, pleased to have secured the attention of the emperor, said with a grin: 'He has distributed today a vast number of new clothes.' The emperor, with the sweetest possible expression on his face, took this for the silly joke it was, and entered the church in humble devotion, and there behaved himself so reverently that he seemed to have our Lord Jesus Christ Himself before his bodily eyes.

22. It was his habit to go to the baths every Saturday, not for any need there was of it, but because it gave him an opportunity of making presents; for he used to give everything that he took off, except his sword and belt, to his attendants. His liberality

reached even to the lowest grades: insomuch that he once
ordered all his attire to be given to one Stracholf, a glazier, and
a servant of St Gall. When the wandering servants of the soldiers
heard of this, they laid an ambuscade for him on the road and
tried to rob him. Then he cried out: 'What are you doing? You
are using violence to the glazier of the emperor!' They answered:
'You can keep your office but . . .'

NOTES

EINHARD: THE LIFE OF CHARLEMAGNE

WALAHFRID'S PREFACE

1. *Francia*: This is the name of the territory inhabited and ruled over by the Franks. By the eighth century it included all of what is now France, and also lands east of the Rhine corresponding to modern Hesse, Alemannia and Thuringia.

THE LIFE OF CHARLEMAGNE

1. *there are many people ... by writing nothing*: There is an echo here of the preface to the Life of St Martin by Sulpicius Severus. See Carolinne White, *Early Christian Lives* (Penguin Classics).

2. *by the witness of my own eyes*: Einhard also uses this expression, *oculata fide*, in his *Translation of the Relics of Marcellinus and Peter*, III.20. It is found in a letter of Cyprian (died 258) referring to St Paul's ascent to heaven, and in other saints' lives.

3. *you*: Probably Gerward, court librarian of Louis the Pious.

4. *I, a barbarian, with too little training in the language of Rome*: Einhard's mother tongue was German, and he learned his Latin at the monastery of Fulda.

5. *'For people ... of letters'*: Cicero, *Tusculan Disputations* (composed around 45 BC), 1.3.6.

6. *King Childeric ... Pope Stephen*: Childeric III (743–51) was deposed by Pope Zacharias and not by Pope Stephen, according to the Royal Frankish Annals.

7. *flowing hair*: The Merovingian rulers were distinguished by their long hair.

8. *his father Charles*: Charles Martel, mayor of the palace from 714

to 741. Cf. P. Fouracre, *The Age of Charles Martel* (London, 2000).

9. *Poitiers*: The battle of Poitiers was fought in 732.

10. *on the River Berre*: The battle on the Berre was fought in 737.

11. *Pippin ... that king mentioned above*: Pippin and Carloman became kings in 741; Carloman abdicated in 747. Cf. Roger Collins, 'Pippin III as Mayor of the Palace: The Evidence', in M. Becher and J. Jarnut (eds.), *Der Dynastiewechsel von 751: Vorgeschichte, Legitimations strategien und Erinnerung* (Münster, 2004), pp. 75–91.

12. *Mount Soracte*: About 70 kilometres north of Rome.

13. *the monastery of St Benedict ... the religious life*: Monte Cassino, about 130 kilometres south of Rome, is the site of a monastery founded by St Benedict around 529 and refounded in 718. In fact, Carloman died at Vienne, according to the Royal Frankish Annals for 755.

14. *nine years*: 760–68.

15. *he died of oedema at Paris*: On 24 September 768.

16. *when Carloman died*: On 4 December 771, according to the Royal Frankish Annals.

17. *the death of Waifar*: In 768.

18. *He forced Hunold ... in Gascony*: This information derives from the Royal Frankish Annals for 769.

19. *Lupus gave way ... to Charles's power*: This account of Lupus is confirmed by the Royal Frankish Annals for 769 and the Astronomer's Life of Louis the Pious, chapter 2.

20. *war against the Lombards*: The Lombard war began in 773.

21. *war was taken up ... very quickly*: Pippin invaded Italy in 755 and 756, after Pope Stephen II had come to Ponthion to ask for his assistance.

22. *He forced ... all that had been seized from the Romans*: Adalgis fled to Constantinople according to the Royal Frankish Annals for 774.

23. *Rotgaud, the duke of Friuli*: In 776.

24. *set up his son Pippin as king of what he had conquered*: Pippin was made king of Italy at Rome in 781.

25. *... was begun again*: The Saxon war began in 772 and lasted until 804.

26. *faithlessness*: The faithlessness of the Saxons is mentioned in the Royal Frankish Annals, 775–7, 785 and 795.

27. *who lived on both sides of the River Elbe*: Einhard's reference to both banks of the river may reveal his local knowledge.

28. *He moved ... in many groups*: This is recorded by the Royal Frankish Annals in 804, though there had been a similar deportation in 799 and a massacre at Werden in 782.

29. *Charles met the enemy in battle ... between them*: These battles took place in 783. Osning is in the Lippischen forest, the Haase is a tributary of the River Ems and the battle was fought near Osnabrück.

30. *false smiling Fortune*: The reference to Fortune probably derives from Book II of Boethius' *Consolation of Philosophy*.

31. *The Basques were aided ... the unevenness of the land*: The Royal Frankish Annals note that the Franks had more weapons and men. The later history of this battle, as told in the *Song of Roland*, is a major theme in European literature.

32. *Eggihard, the overseer of the king's table*: Einhard is our only source for these names. Eggihard's verse epitaph (*Monumenta Germaniae Historica, Poetae*, I. 109–10) records his death in Spain and gives the date of the battle as 15 August 778.

33. *Anselm, the count of the palace*: Anselm is mentioned in royal charters of 775 and 777.

34. *Roland, the prefect of the Breton March*: Roland is the hero of the *Song of Roland*. His name is not found in the B-class of manuscripts of the Life of Charlemagne. Einhard's account draws on the revised version of the Royal Frankish Annals, which also contrast the Franks and the Basques.

35. *He also conquered the Bretons ... do as he ordered*: The Royal Frankish Annals record campaigns against the Bretons in 786, 799 and 811.

36. *he entered Italy ... a city in Campania*: Charlemagne marched to Italy late in 786.

37. *Arichis ... into his presence*: Arichis, duke of Beneventum, promised to pay an annual tribute of 7,000 gold solidi.

38. *Tassilo*: duke of Bavaria from 748 to 788. In 763 he was accused of abandoning Pippin on his Aquitanian campaign. In 781 he is said to have sworn an oath of submission to Charlemagne at the Worms assembly. In 787 there was an attempt at reconciliation with Charlemagne, but Pope Hadrian imposed an anathema and Charlemagne invaded Bavaria; Tassilo swore an oath of vassalage. Einhard's account follows that in the Royal Frankish Annals, using hindsight to distort the record, as Airlie has shown ('Narratives of Triumph and Rituals of Submission: Charlemagne's Mastering of Bavaria', *Transactions of the Royal Historical Society*, 6th series (1999), pp. 93–119).

39. *The king's valour ... to rebel*: The expedition to the Lech was in 787. Tassilo was deposed in 794.

40. *the Wiltzi*: A Slavic people dwelling between the rivers Elbe and Oder. Alcuin hopes for their conversion in his Letter 6 of 789.

41. *A certain gulf ... towards the east*: The Baltic Sea.

42. *In a single expedition ... what he ordered*: The campaign against the Wiltzi took place in 789. They allied with the Danes in 808.

43. *Apart from the war ... representatives*: Charlemagne led expeditions against the Avars in 791 and 793; Pippin defeated them in battle and captured their treasure in 796. Einhard follows the Royal Frankish Annals, though he may have already been at court in 796.

44. *Only two ... governor of Bavaria*: Alcuin's Letter 198 is an attempt to console Charlemagne for their deaths.

45. *all of Italy ... to lower Calabria*: The length of Italy measured from Aosta is found in the third-century Roman geographer Solinus (*Collectanea* 2.23).

46. *Alfonso ... subject*: Alfonso II, king of Galicia and Asturias (789–842), sent an embassy to Charlemagne in 797.

47. *He had such friendly relations ... his honour and generosity*: Harun-al-Rashid, caliph of Bagdad (786–809).

48. *an elephant ... asked for one*: The elephant, Abul Abaz, died on campaign in 810. See the essay 'Charlemagne, King of Beasts', in Paul Dutton's collection, *Charlemagne's Mustache and Other Cultural Clusters of a Dark Age* (Basingstoke, 2004), pp. 43–68.

49. *Nicephorus, Michael and Leo*: Nicephorus I (802–11), Michael I (811–13) and Leo V (813–20).

50. *five hundred paces long ... at this point*: The bridge, built on Roman foundations, was 750 metres long.

51. *This bridge was destroyed ... in place of wood*: The Royal Frankish Annals record the destruction of the bridge in May 813.

52. *whenever he found them falling to ruin ... obeyed*: Repairs of buildings are mentioned in capitularies of 794, 803, 807 and 809 *Monumenta Germaniae Historica, Capitularia Regnum Francorum*, I. 76, 119, 136, 175; P. D. King, *Charlemagne: Translated Sources* (Kendal, 1987), p. 227).

53. *He also fitted out a fleet ... their piratical practices*: This account draws on the Royal Frankish Annals for 798–813.

54. *and sacked it*: In 813.

55. *the Northmen harried ... coast*: Einhard follows the Royal Frankish Annals for 810.

56. *On Fastrada's death . . . no children*: Fastrada, daughter of Count
     Radulf, died in 794 and Liutgard on 4 June 800.

57. *three*: Some manuscripts say four, adding the name of Madelgard
     (only named in the C class of manuscripts, beginning with Paris
     BNF Latin 10758).

58. *after the death of Hildegard*: Hildegard died on 30 April 783,
     Bertrada on 12 July 783.

59. *the monastery in which she had spent her life*: Gisela was abbess
     of Chelles, just outside Paris until her death in 810.

60. *Charles, his eldest son*: Charles died on 4 December 811.

61. *Pippin . . . king of Italy*: Pippin died on 8 July 810.

62. *Rothrud . . . emperor of the Greeks*: Rothrud died on 6 July 810.

63. *he made friends easily . . . most constantly*: This is what Suetonius
     said of Augustus (*Augustus* 66).

64. *He also had a son . . . the false promise of a kingdom*: Pippin
     was the son of Himiltrude. His conspiracy was in 792.

65. *His body was large and strong*: This is what Suetonius said of
     Tiberius (*Tiberius* 68).

66. *his height was seven times the length of his own foot*: When his
     grave was opened in 1861 his skeleton measured 1.92 metres.
     The Roman emperor Theodosius also had a large body, and was
     unduly tall.

67. *he had fine white hair and a cheerful and attractive face*: This
     corresponds to what Suetonius said of Claudius (*Claudius* 30).

68. *his stomach seemed to project*: According to Suetonius, both
     Nero and Titus had protruding bellies (*Nero* 51; *Titus* 3).

69. *the symmetry of the other parts hid these flaws*: Suetonius says
     this of Augustus (*Augustus* 79).

70. *His health was good . . . fevers*: This is what Suetonius had said
     about Julius Caesar (*Julius* 45).

71. *he would limp on one foot*: Suetonius says that Augustus limped
     on one foot (*Augustus* 80).

72. *he trusted his own judgement . . . boiled meats*: Suetonius says
     that Tiberius rejected the advice of his doctors (*Tiberius* 68).

73. *. . . bathing together*: Alcuin (Letter 262) refers to a question
     which Charlemagne had asked him about the number 153 while
     swimming in the bath at Aachen. Cf. Suetonius on the Emperor
     Titus.

74. *on other days . . . the common people*: The terminology and
     details here are found in Suetonius' account of the dress of Augus-
     tus (*Augustus* 82).

75. *fasting was bad for his health*: Certain church festivals, listed in

the 813 Council of Mainz, were celebrated by fasting, and a fast was ordained after the Spanish defeat in 779.

76. *the hunters*: Hincmar of Reims's treatise *De ordine palatii* records four hunters at the court.

77. *he listened ... to a performer*: According to Suetonius, Augustus liked listening to a performer.

78. *City of God*: Written by St Augustine between 412 and 429 in 22 books. Alcuin quotes from it in his Letter 178 to Charlemagne.

79. *a single drink ... four or five times*: Suetonius tells us that Augustus drank only three times at meals, lay down after lunch and woke three or four times during the night.

80. *verbose*: The Latin word *dicaculus*, which Einhard uses here for someone who talks too much, is found only in the *Scriptores Historiae Augusti*, fictional biographies of the later Caesars from Hadrian (117) to Carinus (who died in 284) and probably composed around the 390s (see *The Lives of the Later Caesars* (Penguin Classics)).

81. *most learned*: The phrase *vir ... doctissimus* was first used of Varro, as noted by Augustine (*City of God* 6. 2), and then by Bede of Alfrid of Northumbria and of Aldhelm *Ecclesiastical History*, 5.12 and 5.18.

82. *railings and portals made of solid bronze*: The bronze railings and the doors at Aachen can still be seen there.

83. *at Jerusalem ... to send money*: Alms for Jerusalem are mentioned in a capitulary of 810 (King, *Charlemagne: Translated Sources*, p. 263).

84. *four times during the whole forty-seven years that he reigned*: In 774, 781, 787 and 800.

85. *two laws*: The Lex Salica and the Lex Ribuaria.

86. *the laws ... should be written down*: Charlemagne ordered the codification of the laws of the Saxons, Thuringians and Frisians.

87. *Wintarmanoth ... Heilagmanoth*: Winter month; The little horn, perhaps the turn of the year; Lent month; Easter month; month of joy; month of ploughing; hay month; month of harvest; wood month; month of the wine harvest; harvest or autumn month; holy month.

88. *the east wind ... the east-north wind Ostnordroni*: The listing of twelve winds from twelve directions was standard: they are mentioned by Isidore, *Etymologies* 13.11.3.

89. *there were frequent eclipses ... for seven days*: There were eclipses of the sun on 16 July 809, a total lunar eclipse on 25 December 809, a partial solar eclipse on 5 June 810, a total

lunar eclipse on 20 June 810, a total solar eclipse on 30 November 810, a total lunar eclipse on 14 December 810 and partial solar eclipses on 14–15 May 812 and 4 May 813.

90. *The portico ... on Ascension Day*: The Royal Frankish Annals record a collapse of the portico on 9 April 817, endangering Louis the Pious, but there is no other record of such a collapse in Charlemagne's reign.

91. *an inscription ... the builder of that church*: The eight-line inscription (perhaps with one line painted on each side of the octagon) adds a distich to a six-line poem by Prosper of Aquitaine. It was edited from Leiden Voss Lat. Q 69, fos. 19r–v, in *Monumenta Germaniae Historica, Poetae*, I. 432; see H. Giersiepen, *Die Inscriften des Aachener Doms* (Wiesbaden, 1992), p. 6.

92. *the third ... and to alms*: The Annals of St Bertin for 842 describe how Lothar took from the Aachen treasury this table, which showed a map of the whole world, the stars and the various movements of the planets, and the signs of the zodiac, and cut it up to divide among his soldiery. See D. M. Deliyannis, 'Charlemagne's Silver Tables: The Ideology of an Imperial Capital', *Early Medieval Europe*, 12 (2003), pp. 159–77. The image of the city of Rome may well have been a personification rather than a map.

93. *Hildebald ... Waltgaud*: Respectively, archbishops of Cologne, Mainz, Salzburg, Reims, Besançon, Lyons and Arles, and bishops of Orleans, Amiens, Basle and Liège.

94. *Fredugis ... Irmino*: Respectively, abbots of St Martin's at Tours, Lorsch, St Riquier and St Germain des Près in Paris.

95. *Wala ... Meginhard*: Wala, Charlemagne's cousin, was later abbot of Corbie and adviser to Louis the Pious; Otulf was probably a Bavarian count; Burchard is called *comes stabuli* in the Royal Frankish Annals; Meginhard was sent as an envoy to the king of the Danes in 810.

NOTKER THE STAMMERER:
THE DEEDS OF CHARLEMAGNE

THE FIRST BOOK

1. *when he had destroyed ... the Romans*: See Daniel 2: 31–8.
2. *two Scots from Ireland*: Scotia was the name for Ireland, found in Isidore's *Etymologies* and in Notker's *Martyrology*.
3. *Clement*: Clemens Scottus, the Irish author of an *Ars Grammatica*, taught at the courts of Charlemagne and his son, Louis the Pious.
4. *< ... >*: All the manuscripts have a gap for the name of the second Irishman. He was perhaps the Irishman Cadac-Andreas who was at the court of Charlemagne and is the target of two poems by Theodulph of Orleans.
5. *Alcuin*: The Northumbrian Alcuin (*c.* 735–804) first came to the court of Charlemagne in 786 and was with Charlemagne at Aachen 794–6. He taught grammar and rhetoric. See the article by Donald Bullough in the *Oxford Dictionary of National Biography*.
6. *He gave him the abbey ... those who flocked to him*: Alcuin was made abbot of St Martin's in Tours in 796.
7. *His teaching ... Romans or Athenians*: Cf. Alcuin, Letter 170, and Édouard Jeauneau, *Translatio studii: The Transmission of Learning. A Gilsonian Theme*, Etienne Gilson Series 18 (Toronto, 1995).
8. *make up for your idleness by eager effort*: The expression is used in Charlemagne's preface to the *Homiliary* of Paul the Deacon.
9. *an excellent secretary and writer for his chapel*: The royal chapel was also the chancery.
10. *the cappa of St Martin ... to crush their enemies*: The account of St Martin's cloak is taken from Walahfrid Strabo, *Libellus de exordiis et incrementis quarundam in observationibus ecclesiasticis rerum*, ed. and trans. A. Hartung Correa (Leiden, 1996), p. 192.
11. *'Do you think ... that long journey?'*: Isidore's *Etymologies* 2.29.8 gives the definition of riches as a long provision for a short life.
12. *immutable in his counsel*: Hebrews 6: 17.
13. *my glory and my refuge*: Psalm 30: 2–3 (Vulgate).

14. *'Heavy with the banquet, drowned in drink and buried by wine'*:
    Virgil, *Aeneid* 3.630.
15. *looking from the palace gallery*: See Song of Songs 2:9.
16. *The precentor*: Notker's term *paraphonista* is found in *Ordo
    Romanus* I. 43, an account of papal ceremonial at Rome through-
    out the liturgical year, and in *Ordo Romanus*, xxvii.70. Both
    these texts were known at St Gall.
17. *My master G.*: Grimald, abbot of St Gall 841–72. He was not a
    pupil of Alcuin, nor did Alcuin teach in Italy.
18. *Pope Stephen*: Notker's error. Charlemagne was not anointed by
    Pope Stephen.
19. *'In those days ... of him that is a Jew'*: Zechariah 8: 23.
20. *Pope Leo ... succeeded Stephen*: Leo III was pope from 796 to
    816.
21. *'If I send ... as you desire'*: For a discussion of Notker's account
    of the spread of Roman chant in the Frankish realms, see S. K.
    Rankin, 'Ways of Telling Stories', in Graeme M. Boone (ed.),
    Essays in Medieval Music in Honor of David Hughes (Cam-
    bridge, Mass., 1995), pp. 371–94, and the literature cited there.
22. *Drogo, bishop of Metz*: Drogo was bishop of Metz from 823 to
    855.
23. *Metensian*: Metz is mentioned as a chief centre for chant in
    some texts of Charlemagne's *Capitulary* of 805, and in Paul the
    Deacon's account of Chrodegang in his *History of the Bishops
    of Metz*. The same story is told in John the Deacon's Life of
    Gregory the Great, II.9. The St Gall manuscript of John's Life
    was copied by Notker; cf. Rankin, 'Ways of Telling Stories',
    pp. 373–4, with plate 1. See also M. Claussen, *The Reform
    of the Frankish Church: Chrodegang of Metz and the* Regula
    Canonicorum *in the Eighth Century* (Cambridge, 2004),
    pp. 263–76, and *L'Art du chantre carolingien* (Paris, 2004).
24. *... it is called Mettisc*: In one of the manuscripts the text con-
    tinues: 'The most pious emperor also ordered Peter, the singer
    who had come to reside with him, to reside for a while in the
    monastery of St Gall. There too Charles established the chanting
    as it is today, with an authentic antiphoner, and gave most careful
    instructions, being always a warm champion of St Gall, that the
    Roman method of singing should be both taught and learned.
    He gave to the monastery also much money and many lands,
    Massino and Röthis and others: he also gave a reliquary with
    relics, made of solid gold and gems, which is called the Shrine of
    Charles.'

25. *he was following the Lord's command . . . at an earlier hour than usual*: See Leviticus 23: 32.

26. *the maxim of the wise man . . . particularly foolish*: Ecclesiastes 7:17.

27. *Udalric*: Count Udalric held lands in the Linzgau until his death in 809. MacLean suggests that there is also a reference here to Udalric IV, count in the Linzgau, Argengau, Reingau and Alpgau.

28. *Vainglorious*: Notker's term *cenodoxiae* derives from the fifth-century monastic writer John Cassian.

29. *my lord emperor Charles*: The emperor Charles the Fat. Cf. MacLean, *Kingship and Politics in the Late Ninth Century*.

30. *'He that desires the office of a bishopric desires good work'*: 1 Timothy 3: 1.

31. *Recho*: Bishop of Strasbourg 783–815.

32. *East Francia*: That is, New Francia, the kingdom of the Eastern Franks, east of the Rhine. In chapter 23 below, Notker speaks of 'Old Francia'.

33. *which I shudder to describe*: An echo of Virgil, *Aeneid* 2.204.

34. *Sigolsheim*: This town near Colmar in the valley of Kaysersberg still produces excellent wine, notably Mambourg.

35. *he washed the night away*: A quotation from the Roman poet Persius, *Satire* 2.16

36. *hobgoblin*: Notker's term is used by Augustine (*City of God*, 8.11) for wicked men who have become demons and attack the living and the dead.

37. *Bromius or Dis*: That is, Bacchus and Pluto, the gods of wine and of the underworld respectively. The deities Bromius and Dis are mentioned by the fifth-century Christian Latin poet Prudentius in his poem *Contra Symmachum*, which Notker will have known.

38. *laying a snare in the way that we walk*: Psalm 140: 10 (Vulgate).

39. *rumour, of all evils the most swift*: Virgil, *Aeneid* 4.174.

40. *'Thou art Peter . . . shall not prevail against it'*: Matthew 16: 18.

41. *'. . . falsely laid against me'*: Two manuscripts include the following addition: 'Then many of the prisoners asked to be allowed to swear upon the tomb of St Peter that they also were innocent of the charge laid against them. But the pope knew their falseness and said to Charles: "Do not, I pray you, unconquered servant of God, give assent to their cunning; for well they know that St Peter is always ready to forgive. But seek among the tombs of the martyrs the stone upon which is written the name of St Pancras, that boy of thirteen years; and if they will swear to

you in his name you may know that you have them fast." It was done as the pope ordered. And when many people drew near to take the oath upon this tomb, straight away some fell back dead and some were seized by the devil and went mad.'

42. ... *perpetual banishment*: Notker's account of the blinding of Leo and the coronation of Charlemagne draws on the life of Leo III in the *Liber Pontificalis*. Cf. Raymond Davis, *The Lives of the Eighth-Century Popes*, Translated Texts for Historians, 13 (Liverpool, 1992), pp. 173–230.

43. *as the Egyptians once afflicted the people of God*: Exodus 2: 11.

44. *the mass of flames*: see Virgil *Georgics* 1.473.

45. *'if riches increase set not his heart upon them'*: Psalm 61: 11 (Vulgate).

46. *The arches of the great bridge ... destroyed it*: The bridge at Mainz was burned in 813, as Einhard notes (see chapters 17 and 32), and again destroyed in 886.

47. *from the windows of his chamber ... free from observation*: See M. de Jong, 'Charlemagne's Balcony: Biblical Commentary, Court Sociability, and Carolingian Palace Architecture'; *New Directions in Early Medieval History*, 2 (2008); J. Nelson, 'Aachen as a Place of Power', in M. de Jong and F. Theuws with C. van Rhijn, *Topographies of Power in the Early Middle Ages*, The Transformation of the Roman World 6 (Leiden, 2001), pp. 217–42.

48. *the adversary of St Anthony*: Athanasius' Life of Antony tells of his encounter with a giant in chapter 38.

49. *Polyphemus*: The one-eyed giant Cyclops who imprisoned Ulysses and his men. Notker will have known about him from Virgil, *Aeneid* 3.588 ff. rather than Homer's *Odyssey*.

50. *There was a deacon ... did public penance*: On this story, see F. Lošek, 'Die Spinne in der Kirchendecke – eine St Galler Klostergeschichte (Notker, Gesta Karoli 1,32)', in A. Scharer and G. Scheibelreiter, *Historiographie im frühen Mittelalter* (Munich, 1994), 253–61, who shows that the deacon was homosexual.

51. *for Moses the lawgiver ... 'slow of speech, and of a slow tongue'*: Exodus 4: 10.

52. *'among them that are born of women there hath not arisen a greater' than he*: Matthew 11: 11.

53. *He allowed John ... though weak women paid many visits to it*: John 20: 5.

54. *'Unto everyone that hath shall be given'*: Matthew 25: 29.

THE SECOND BOOK

1. *Julian, whom God hated*: Julian is described in this way in the *Historia Tripartita* XVII.

2. *'The land of the Avars ... from one to the other'*: The Avar Hring, the series of concentric ring-shaped fortifications described by Notker, is first mentioned in the Royal Frankish Annals for 796 and seems to have been the term for their capital. See W. Pohl, 'The Regia and the Hring – Barbarian Places of Power', in de Jong and Theuws with van Rhijn, *Topographies of Power in the Early Middle Ages*, pp. 439–66. Avar treasure is to be found in the Hungarian National Museum in Budapest.

3. *They concealed their indignation ... of the enemy*: For a discussion of military status in the ninth century which uses this story, see K. Leyser, 'Early Medieval Canon Law and the Beginning of Knighthood', in his *Communications and Power in Medieval Europe: The Carolingian and Ottonian Centuries*, ed. T. Reuter, (London, 1994), pp. 51–72.

4. *Bishop Heito ... to Constantinople*: Bishop Heito of Basle (806–23), who signed Charlemagne's will, went on an embassy to Constantinople in 811.

5. *an army like that which drove back the Syrians and Assyrians out of Samaria*: 2 Kings 6: 14

6. *'Kings of the earth ... praise the name of the Lord'*: Psalm 148: 11–12.

7. *and he, hidden nearby, was so pleased ... 'contrivit'*: Other manuscripts read: 'psalms with the same melody and same subject matter as "Veterem hominem" and the following words in our missal. Thereupon the emperor ordered one of his chaplains, who understood the Greek language, to adopt that psalm in Latin to the same melody, and to take special care that a separate syllable corresponded to every separate note, so that the Latin and Greek should resemble one another as far as the nature of the two languages allowed.'

8. *the bellows of oxhide*: See Virgil, *Georgics* 4.171.

9. *every kind of organ ... cymbal*: For an account of classical and medieval organs, see the article 'Organ' by P. Williams in the *New Grove Dictionary of Music and Musicians*, 2nd edn. (Oxford, 2003).

10. *But when the Morn ... Phoebus' torch*: Virgil, *Aeneid* 4. 585

and 4.6. The first of these lines is quoted by Isidore, *Etymologies*, 1.37.14, as an example of periphrasis.

11. *Isambard*: A Count Isambard owned lands in Thurgau from 774 and endowed St Gall. He is last recorded in 806. Warin is mentioned in the Life of St Gall, and in St Gall charters from the period 754–72.

12. *an elephant*: The elephant, Abul Abaz, is mentioned in the Royal Frankish Annals and by Einhard (chapter 17).

13. *Harun*: Harun-al-Rashid. See n. 47 to Einhard (p. 120):

14. *Marmarican*: Marmarica is apparently between Egypt and Syria, but Notker is being exotic. Marmarican Lions and Numidian bears are both mentioned in Pliny's *Natural History*. 'Africans' here refers to the North African coast.

15. *Spanish purple*: See Virgil, *Aeneid* 9.582.

16. *the strongest heir to that name*: According to St Jerome, Aaron, as Harun is rendered in Latin, means 'mountain of strength'.

17. *'Either the Parthian shall drink the Arar or Germany the Tigris'*: Virgil, *Eclogues* 1.62.

18. *your father*: On Louis the German (emperor 843–76), see E. J. Goldberg, *Struggle for Empire: Kingship and Conflict under Louis the German, 817–876* (Ithaca, NY, 2006). The meeting with Charlemagne could have taken place in 813.

19. *the Life of St Ambrose*: In chapter 3 of his Life of St Ambrose, Paulinus tells of the prophecy made over the young Ambrose: 'If the lad lives, he will be someone great.'

20. *abbot Hartmut*: Abbot of St Gall 872–83, when he resigned and lived as a hermit.

21. *King Louis . . . all his nobles*: Charters of Louis for St Gall issued in February and April 873 have survived.

22. *once only . . . the most absolute necessity*: When he killed the rebel Stellingas is 842.

23. *like St Martin . . . face to face with Him*: See Sulpicius Severus, Life of St Martin, chapter 26.

24. *the cathedral*: The church of St Peter in Regensburg.

25. *he followed the customs of those he was with*: Louis the German's piety is recorded in the Annals of Fulda (trans. T. Reuter, Manchester, 1992). On his death he was called *pius* at St Gall.

26. *He built new oratories . . . at Frankfurt and Regensburg*: The chapel of the Saviour at Frankfurt was consecrated in 852; the chapel of Our Lady at Regensburg is mentioned in a diploma of 875.

27. *'A king that sitteth in the throne of judgement scattereth away all evil with His eyes'*: Proverbs 20: 8.

28. *'measured with the sword'*: An echo of 2 Samuel 8:2.

29. *'What portion have we in David . . . of Jesse?'*: 1 Kings 12: 16.

30. *a monastery . . . now destroyed*: The monastery of Prüm, destroyed by the Vikings in 882.

31. *the race of Anak*: These men, accounted giants, are mentioned in Deuteronomy 2: 10.

32. *He might prove Israel*: Judges 3: 4.

33. *'trying to move against the cunning of the stream'*: Ecclesiasticus 4: 32 (Vulgate).

34. *Godfrid . . . for his home*: Godfrid I invaded Frisia and not the Moselle region, but his son Godfrid III in 885 targeted Coblenz and Andernach.

35. *Holofernes*: The Assyrian general sent by Nebuchadnezzar to attack the Israelites. He was slain by Judith, as described in the biblical book of Judith in the Apocrypha.

36. *The sword of your brother Carloman will help*: Carloman king of Bavaria died in 880.

37. *Arnulf*: Arnulf of Carinthia (reigned as king of East Francia 887–99), crowned emperor in 896, was the son of Carloman.

38. *Many people . . . the birthdays of the apostles*: The text derives from Ephesians 2: 19. Aurelian of Reomé records that it was sung on the feast of the apostles. It was also sung as a responsory at the second nocturn of All Saints.

39. *Bede . . . has devoted nearly a whole book to him*: In fact, Bede makes a passing mention of Pippin in Book V, chapters 10–11, of the *Ecclesiastical History*.

40. *he married the daughter of Desiderius, king of the Lombards*: In 770.

41. *. . . in the hope of gain*: Pavia was captured in July 774 after a siege which lasted for ten months.

42. *the city of Friuli . . . Forum Julii*: Cividale del Friuli was the seat of the patriarch of Aquilea. Charlemagne went there in 776.

43. *the cloak which St Martin wore . . . divine approval*: The story of St Martin dividing his cloak is told in Sulpicius Severus, *Dialogi* 2. 1.

44. *Pavia . . . beyond the sea*: For Venetian merchants at Pavia, see the Life of St Gerald of Aurillac, 1. 27.

45. *his most terrible censure*: Both Alcuin (Letter 231) and Einhard (chapter 23) record Charlemagne's dislike of costly clothing.

46. *'Look to the rock whence ye were hewn'*: Isaiah 51: 1.

47. *When the kings of the Northmen . . . 'Would that our kings held gold and silver so cheap and iron so precious'*: This story probably refers to the Danish embassy of 873. Regino of Prüm, in his Chronicle for 876, also records Louis's preference for the strength of iron rather than the glint of gold. See S. MacLean, *The Chronicle of Regino of Prüm* (Manchester, 2008).

48. *'If there were no Trinity . . . Holy Spirit'*: Augustine, *De Trinitate* 15.28, quoting Matthew 28: 19.

49. *'For as many . . . put on Christ'*: Galatians 3: 27.

50. *'So many of us as were baptized . . . into His death'*: Romans 6: 3.

51. *'Crucifying the Son of God afresh and putting Him to an open shame!'*: Hebrews 6: 6.

52. *Achitophel*: Counsellor to King David, who joined in the rebellion of Absalom. When his advice was not taken he hanged himself (2 Samuel 15–17).

53. *Anselm*: Perhaps Archbishop Anselm of Milan (814–22), mentioned in Thegan's Life of Louis the Pious chapter 22.

54. *food and clothing*: T. Reuter, 'Plunder and Tribute in the Carolingian Empire', in his Medieval Polities and Modern Mentalities (Cambridge, 2006), p. 237

55. *according to the Acts of the Apostles . . . that lacked*: See Acts 4: 34.

PENGUIN CLASSICS

THE RISE OF THE ROMAN EMPIRE
POLYBIUS

> 'If history is deprived of the truth,
> we are left with nothing but an idle, unprofitable tale'

In writing his account of the relentless growth of the Roman Empire, the Greek statesman Polybius (*c.* 200–118 BC) set out to help his fellow-countrymen understand how their world came to be dominated by Rome. Opening with the Punic War in 264 BC, he vividly records the critical stages of Roman expansion: its campaigns throughout the Mediterranean, the temporary setbacks inflicted by Hannibal and the final destruction of Carthage in 146 BC. An active participant in contemporary politics, as well as a friend of many prominent Roman citizens, Polybius was able to draw on a range of eyewitness accounts and on his own experiences of many of the central events, giving his work immediacy and authority.

Ian Scott-Kilvert's translation fully preserves the clarity of Polybius' narrative. This substantial selection of the surviving volumes is accompanied by an introduction by F. W. Walbank, which examines Polybius' life and times, and the sources and technique he employed in writing his history.

Translated by Ian Scott-Kilvert
Selected with an introduction by F. W. Walbank

PENGUIN CLASSICS

THE CAMPAIGNS OF ALEXANDER
ARRIAN

'His passion was for glory only, and in that he was insatiable'

Although written over four hundred years after Alexander's death, Arrian's *Campaigns of Alexander* is the most reliable account of the man and his achievements we have. Arrian's own experience as a military commander gave him unique insights into the life of the world's greatest conqueror. He tells of Alexander's violent suppression of the Theban rebellion, his total defeat of Persia, and his campaigns through Egypt, India and Babylon – establishing new cities and destroying others in his path. While Alexander emerges from this record as an unparalleled and charismatic leader, Arrian succeeds brilliantly in creating an objective and fully rounded portrait of a man of boundless ambition, who was exposed to the temptations of power and worshipped as a god in his own lifetime.

Aubrey de Sélincourt's vivid translation is accompanied by J. R. Hamilton's introduction, which discusses Arrian's life and times, his synthesis of other classical sources and the composition of Alexander's army. This edition also includes maps, a list for further reading and a detailed index.

Translated by Aubrey de Sélincourt

Revised, with a new introduction and notes by J. R. Hamilton

THE STORY OF PENGUIN CLASSICS

Before 1946 ... 'Classics' are mainly the domain of academics and students; readable editions for everyone else are almost unheard of. This all changes when a little-known classicist, E. V. Rieu, presents Penguin founder Allen Lane with the translation of Homer's *Odyssey* that he has been working on in his spare time.

1946 Penguin Classics debuts with *The Odyssey*, which promptly sells three million copies. Suddenly, classics are no longer for the privileged few.

1950s Rieu, now series editor, turns to professional writers for the best modern, readable translations, including Dorothy L. Sayers's *Inferno* and Robert Graves's unexpurgated *Twelve Caesars*.

1960s The Classics are given the distinctive black covers that have remained a constant throughout the life of the series. Rieu retires in 1964, hailing the Penguin Classics list as 'the greatest educative force of the twentieth century.'

1970s A new generation of translators swells the Penguin Classics ranks, introducing readers of English to classics of world literature from more than twenty languages. The list grows to encompass more history, philosophy, science, religion and politics.

1980s The Penguin American Library launches with titles such as *Uncle Tom's Cabin*, and joins forces with Penguin Classics to provide the most comprehensive library of world literature available from any paperback publisher.

1990s The launch of Penguin Audiobooks brings the classics to a listening audience for the first time, and in 1999 the worldwide launch of the Penguin Classics website extends their reach to the global online community.

The 21st Century Penguin Classics are completely redesigned for the first time in nearly twenty years. This world-famous series now consists of more than 1300 titles, making the widest range of the best books ever written available to millions – and constantly redefining what makes a 'classic'.

The Odyssey continues ...

The best books ever written

PENGUIN (🐧) CLASSICS

SINCE 1946